D1520022

NOISE AND PRICES

Noise and Prices

A. A. WALTERS

CLARENDON PRESS · OXFORD
1975

Oxford University Press, Ely House, London W. 1

GLASGOW NEW YORK TORONTO MELBOURNE WELLINGTON
CAPE TOWN IBADAN NAIROBI DAR ES SALAAM LUSAKA ADDIS ABABA
DELHI BOMBAY CALCUTTA MADRAS KARACHI LAHORE DACCA
KUALA LUMPUR SINGAPORE HONG KONG TOKYO

ISBN 0 19 828197 8

Printed in Northern Ireland at The Universities Press, Belfast

To
Paddie

Preface

CONCERN with the quality of life and the ecological balance has recently dominated much discussion of public policy. Air pollution, visual intrusion and noise have been with us for many decades but it is only during the past five years or so that these issues have come to play a crucial role in the decisions of authorities. It is no accident that the loudest and most effective voices of protest have been heard in the countries which have relatively high incomes; after all it is only the relatively affluent who have both the taste and the income to support their search for a "high quality environment"; there are no constraints on the making of smoke or noise in Ankara or Calcutta. But in the Western democracies the widespread view among the influential middle classes that the quality of life has deteriorated in recent years, whether right or wrong, has moved many a politician to pledge that he will be a faithful defender of the "environment."

The need for some degree of objectivity in dealing with such an emotional issue as the environment is obvious. This study is an attempt to analyse one particular bad environmental feature—the noise of aircraft—in terms of people's economic behaviour. In this study, we are not concerned with the effect of aircraft noise on people's physiological or psychological make-up—except in so far as these changes are manifest in the prices which people pay for goods and services on the market. Only economic consequences are traced and evaluated. The economic effects of aircraft noise are, however, not crystal clear in theory and they become quite hazy when one examines the empirical evidence.

My interest in the economics of noise was stimulated largely by becoming a member of the Roskill Commission in 1968.[1]

---

[1] *The Commission on the Third London Airport*, chairman Lord Justice Roskill.

The Commission were charged with the task of carrying out a cost-benefit study in the search for a site for a third airport. Aircraft noise was one of the important factors which the Commission were required to take into account. There was obviously a great incentive to see whether one could represent the differential costs of noise in terms of a money measure so that it could be compared with those costs—such as access expenses and spending on construction—which could be much more readily and acceptably measured in money terms. This therefore was the motivation for the analysis.

The Roskill Commission was fortunate in gathering together a splendid Research Team led by Frank Thompson, the director of research. But the cost-benefit study—although primarily the fruit of the efforts of the Research Team—was much influenced by the Commission itself. The process of enquiry and the production of the research results was very much a social process—and I may add a very pleasant social process. The cut and thrust of free discussion eventually gave rise to what I term the *Roskill Research Team Noise Model*.

But the pressure on the Commission, and so on the Research Team, was to produce figures for the costs of noise. The need was for operational results rather than analytical niceties. Such results were produced and much debated, and it became clear during these debates that there was generally much uncertainty about the theoretical basis of the noise model. The attempt to fill this theoretical vacuum is one of the rationalisations for this study. But more important is the search in the evidence for the empirical regularities or even constants to introduce a seemly order into the chaotic data. The test of a theory is its ability to predict events which are surprising and not hitherto obvious— but above all which are not discredited by the facts. Judgement of the tests and their success must be left to the reader. I am conscious, however, of leaving many important questions unanswered as well as many i's undotted and t's uncrossed. But to wait until all the answers are clear would be to wait for ever; there is *some* rate of time discount on scholarship.

In writing this manuscript I have been continually reminded of the many debts that I owe and alas will never discharge. My obligations to the Roskill Commission and the Research Team extend far beyond the narrow confines of the subject matter of this book. But in developing my ideas on noise and in testing the credibility of economic analysis, Lord Justice Roskill, the Chairman, and Mr. Alfred Goldstein, one of the members of the Commission, played a most important role. The prodigious intelligence which underlay their incisive questioning soon exposed any sloppy economic thinking; furthermore I learned that even the most complicated ideas could be expressed in simple English. (I formed the view that Lord Justice Roskill and Mr. Goldstein were born 'natural' economists—but I am not sure that either would willingly acknowledge what may now be taken to be a sad congenital defect!)

I believe that both Mr. Frank Thompson, the director of the Roskill Research Team and now Director of Research for The Civil Aviation Authority, and I independently arrived at the basic arguments for using house price differentials in the noise evaluation methodology. It was under his guidance that the initial data were collected and he was the source of many of the ideas that produced the Research Team model. The two members of the Team who contributed most to the detailed operational development of the Roskill Noise model were Messrs. S. V. Abrahams (now with the C.A.A.), and A. D. J. Flowerdew (now at The London School of Economics). The difficulties which they encountered in fitting the pieces of the model together, in getting suitable data, and in debugging the programmes were formidable. It is a fitting testimony to their ingenuity and application that the model ran successfully and produced the results on time.

During the Stage V hearings of the Roskill Commission the noise evaluation methods were subject to searching enquiry. It was at this stage that I realised the need for an economic analysis of noise to provide a more rational and empirically sound basis for the propositions of the Research Team's model. The most influential witness was Mr. S. P. D. Plowden (METRA)—who, although I believe mistaken in his fundamental assertion, shed a great deal of light on the weaknesses of the model. It was Mr. Plowden more than anyone who induced me to develop the various models of chapters 3 and 4 to answer the specific charges he so ably presented.

I am most indebted to the Urban Institute of Washington D.C., for providing me with the resources to enable me to review the data collected in the United States and Canada. Much of the first draft of this manuscript was written during the summer of 1972 when the Institute provided me with such excellent facilities that writing became a pleasure. Dr. Peter Brown and Richard Wagner of the Institute read the manuscript and made useful contributions. Mr. Robert Spaeth contributed almost all the material on the various legal cases in the United States.

In the last stages Professor Yoram Barzel of the University of Washington read the manuscript and found a number of errors. Diane Giles and Sheila Collins spent many hours typing the manuscript, checking the proofs and correcting my frequent slips. I am grateful but must claim the usual responsibility for any that remain.

One final word. The methods of analysis that are developed here are applied particularly to aircraft noise. But their range of applicability is much wider. In principle they can be applied to any other localised amenity or disamenity. Indeed, the methods have been applied with some success in the analysis of the environmental effects of city roads.[2] Since environmental pollution varies significantly from one locality to another there is some reason to believe that many more useful areas of application are to be unearthed. This book may be viewed as a prologue to such environmental economics.

September, 1973   A. A. WALTERS

---

[2] A. D. J. Flowerdew and A. Hammond "City Roads and the Environment", *Regional Studies*, Vol. 6, 1973 (Pergamon).

CONTENTS

CHAPTER I

An Introduction and Summary

AIRCRAFT NOISE AS A PUBLIC BAD

NOISE is normally treated as a form of wholesale pollution, like an inescapable blanket of suffocation laid over society. In many respects this is not a bad analogy. A quiet environment is not a private property right just as clean air is not an appropriated commodity. And just as private and publicly controlled industries have made the air foul in the pursuit of private gain, so the airlines have destroyed the peace of communities lying under their flight paths. Valuable services, clean air and a quiet life, have been expropriated by industrial and transport corporations. Furthermore, it is unusual for the corporations to have to *pay* for the privilege of polluting the air or assaulting our ears.[1]

The reasons for the lack of property rights in clean air and a quiet life are partly accidents of history but also partly the difficulty of defining and measuring the quality of the service. What is clean air and how can one define quiet? Even now there is much controversy about suitable definitions of these concepts.

But there is one other peculiar feature of these "bads", pollution and noise—a very large number of people suffer them. If there were only one or two people affected then it would be easy to derive mutually agreed compensation arrangements. But when the number is very large the obstacles to any such agreement become insurmountable. Each resident will have an incentive to play "hard-to-get" and to hold out for the maximum offer. The purchase of land for highway or railroad construction illustrates the difficulties of arriving at any voluntary arrangement with one purchaser against so many sellers. The state usually enacts laws of compulsory purchase with "fair market value" compensation. Those who would argue that the noise problem is best left to the parties concerned, noise makers and sufferers, to arrive at a mutual contract in a

---

[1] The general doctrine however, is, *cujus est solum ejus est usque ad coelum.*

free market thus have no good precedents to appeal to. State intervention has been normally thought necessary.

The other question of some importance is whether noise is a public good like defence. All of us have to enjoy the same degree of security produced by the defence budget. No British citizen, for example, can legally opt out of supporting the British Army in Ulster; he must pay his taxes to cover the whole defence package whether he likes it or not. With aircraft noise however (and to a lesser extent pollution), it is possible to avoid much of the din. I can choose to reside off the flight paths in the quiet areas or I can buy a house just off the edge of the runway. As far as a residence is concerned one can choose from a continuous spectrum of noise—from very quiet to pure hell—according to the distance from the runway and flight paths. In principle those who are sensitive to noise would choose a quiet place of employment. Employers such as universities would be induced to locate in quiet areas if they wished to employ sensitive people. And sensitive people, of course, give up many opportunities for both employment and residence in order to buy quiet.

Two points emerge from this discussion. First, aircraft noise is not a ubiquitous public good—like foreign aid or the defence umbrella—which all of us must buy at the amount specified by the government. Even with quite small communities one has the option of buying peace at a price. (In practice one buys peace as a joint product—with a piece of real estate or perhaps with a job.) Aircraft noise is a local and not a ubiquitous phenomenon. A second point is that one can buy a little or a lot of quiet since noise is more or less a continuum as far as human reaction is concerned. Although it is often convenient analytically to assume that houses are either noisy or quiet— and we shall do so later on—it is a travesty of the facts of the case. There are no fixed proportions between houses and noise. In practice one can nicely adjust one's house purchase to the amount of noise one is prepared to tolerate for the other advantages so obtained.[2] We can conceive then of the good "freedom from aircraft noise" or in short "quiet" as the quantity which is scarce and for which people will be prepared to pay.

---

[2] All this of course presupposes that the individuals acquire knowledge of the noisy areas, both existing and potential. We return to this later.

IMPLICIT MARKETS

This study will concentrate on the analysis of the price paid for quiet and the quantity of quiet which people buy at those prices. There is, however, no institutionally organized market for quiet—it cannot be found in the Yellow Pages. There are no reported quantity and price-of-quiet data available. Quiet is not a nicely defined and specified right which can be found in a contract. Nor is quiet guaranteed by law—although the grossest violations do call for and elicit some redress. All one can get is a "high probability of a peaceful environment" or some other such expectation.

The fact that there is no explicit market for this expectation of quiet does not mean that a market does not exist. It merely means that the market for quiet becomes implicit. In the most obvious sense the quantity of quiet that we buy is largely associated with the decisions about the purchase of a house or where we decide to rent a hereditament. Thus if we wish to enjoy perfect peace from aircraft noise we would buy a house far from present or expected flight paths. The premium which one would have to pay on such a quiet house, compared with a house lying under the flight paths, would measure the expenditure one thought worthwhile to lay out for a quiet life—or at least for a reasonable expectation of peaceful residential conditions.

THE MEASUREMENT OF NOISE NUISANCE (CHAPTER 2)

Such observed expenditures on quiet, however, do not tell us either the price of quiet or the quantity of quiet purchased. In order to decompose the expenditure on quiet into the price and quantity components we must adopt a measure of quantity of quiet. This is the task of chapter 2. Instead of measuring the quantity of 'good', freedom from aircraft noise, we measure the 'bad', aircraft noise itself—and so follow the well-developed techniques of acoustical scientists. The various methods that have been developed for measuring the degree of annoyance caused by various patterns of aircraft noise all give broadly similar results. They are all combinations of the peak noisiness and the number of occasions on which noise is heard. Simple

and reliable transformations have been calculated so that one
may switch from one scale to another.

But it may be claimed that the really important issue about
such quantitative measures of noise is whether they can be
taken as merely *ordinal* magnitudes or whether they can be
identified as *cardinal* measures. The method of derivation of
such measures as the Noise Number Index (NNI) and the
Composite Noise Rating (CNR) suggests that they can be
regarded only as ordinal measures—so that one can conclude
only that an NNI of 50 is worse than one of 45 which is again
worse than one of 40; one cannot infer that a change from 40 to
45 is *just as bad* as an increase from 45 to 50. To construct a
cardinal scale of units of noise one must have additional information such as expenditure and price data. For the characteristic feature of the quantity measure of all economic goods sold
on the same market is that units are identical in that they
command the same price.[3] This is the appropriate *economic*
definition of quantity. As we shall show in chapter 6, over most
of the relevant range the NNI and CNR happen to have the
characteristics of economic quantities with arbitrary units of
measurement. The evidence suggests that, with the same
price per NNI or CNR unit of quiet and with the same
income, the householder pays as much to go from 45 to 40 NNI
as from 50 to 45. Thus it makes sense to analyse unit movements of NNI and CNR as though they were cardinal magnitudes.[4]

THE HOUSEHOLD DEMAND FOR QUIET
(CHAPTER 3)

It is convenient to begin the analysis of house prices and
noise by assuming that there are no frictions in the system and
that movement costs are zero. A householder may then buy as
much residential quiet as he wishes at the going price. If that
price varies one may generate a demand for quiet by the individual householder on the usual assumption that all other

[3] Quantity discounts in a competitive market normally reflect the lower
administrative costs of having only one transaction instead of lots of little
ones; the price per unit of commodity excluding transactions costs is constant.

[4] It is fortunate that one does not have to make awkward transformations
to get an appropriate quantity unit of quiet—but further evidence on both
expenditures and other measures of noise may well show that more refinement
is needed. We are only at the beginning of this inquiry into the price of quiet.

prices remain constant. Thus it is possible to calculate the amount the householder would be willing to pay in order to enjoy a lower price of quiet—or alternatively one can measure the householder's valuation of a given change in the amount of noise.

In practice, however, the fact that quiet is an attribute of the house and cannot be bought separately on the market (insulation is only a very partial offset to a house in a noisy area) causes complications in analysis. Even with zero movement costs, it is clear that owners get attached to their property; a house becomes 'personalized' and in general worth more than the price it would command on the market. This "surplus" which an owner enjoys in his existing property is closely analogous to Marshall's consumer surplus, and can be defined as the minimum amount he would require over and above the market price of the property in order to sell and move. This is a measure of the *compensation* he would require in order to move. Alternatively, the authorities could require him to move and offer the market price for his house, then melt a little and allow him to buy back the right to stay where he is—the maximum amount he would offer would measure his *willingness to pay* to stay put. We know also that the assumption of zero moving costs is absurd. In fact movement and transactions cost together with the differential surplus introduce much friction into the process by which the market adjusts to a new price of quiet or to a new source of noise nuisance.

Finally we develop a simple rule to set out the conditions under which a householder will find it to be in his interests to move. Such a rule was first developed by the Research Team of the Roskill Commission. A new source of noise in an area hitherto more or less quiet will induce a householder to move if his valuation of the expected noise nuisance exceeds the expected loss he would incur by moving. Otherwise he will stay put.

THE MARKET FOR HOUSING AND THE COSTS OF NOISE (CHAPTER 4)

The market demand for quiet is obtained by summing the individual demand curves for quiet. Similarly the sum of the householder demands for noisy houses and for quiet houses gives the respective market demands. But different people have different tastes for their environmental conditions. One would expect people to express their tastes by the amount of quiet they purchase at given prices—the imperturbables would buy little or nothing whereas the sensitive soul would buy a lot. However, it is convenient first to analyse the case where quiet is simply an *attribute*—an all-or-nothing proposition. Either one buys a noisy house or a quiet one. A man's taste for quiet is measured by the amount he would be willing to pay for a quiet house. Indeed one way of analysing the effects of a change in the quantity of noisy houses is to find the derived demand for quiet; and many readers may find it more convenient to think in terms of the derived demand curve.

The condition of equilibrium is that the prices of noisy and quiet houses be such that the existing supplies are just equal to the quantities demanded. Normally, one would expect the price of the quiet house to exceed that of a noisy one. An increase in the supply of noise will increase the number of noisy houses and reduce the number of quiet houses and should therefore increase the price of quiet houses and reduce the price of noisy ones. The value of the noise differential would increase. In most practical cases one may take it that the changes in supply are sufficiently small relative to the total size of the market for it to be possible to take the noise differential as given. This approximation is quite convenient for any problem involving only small changes.

Such an attribute model, however, has serious disadvantages. It does not enable one to assimilate and use the information generated by the fact that householders can and do nicely adjust the amount of quiet they purchase according to their taste. So we develop a simple general equilibrium model in order to explore the implications of varying the relative quantities of quiet and other goods. Ignoring movement and adjustment costs one can identify the fraction of income that a household spends on quiet with a 'taste for quiet' parameter in the utility function of the household. In the special case where the utility function is a Cobb–Douglas type the variation in the relative supply of quiet, although affecting the relative price of quiet, does not affect the level of individual expenditure on quiet. This model is inherently more plausible than the attribute model. It also enables us neatly to interpret the evidence of expenditures on quiet.

One of the least-understood processes is the dynamics of the adjustment of the economy to a new noise source under conditions where there are movement costs and differential surpluses involved. Although one can derive a simple moving rule as was developed in chapter 3, to put this into a time context is most complex and perplexing. Only the most superficial discussion is attempted here—it is an outline sketch rather than a complete story. I can only plead lack of ability and knowledge to do more.

Much of the discussion of noise is cast in terms of the effect on residents and owners. In a private enterprise system the effects on other institutions such as schools and hospitals would be reflected in the values of their services directly and, if they serve exclusively the noisy areas, in the prices of the noisy properties. But the market does not work this way, or one should more correctly say the market is not allowed to work in such a fashion. Schools and in many cases hospitals are governmental organizations and are financed and administered according to different principles from businesses. It is therefore necessary to add on to the residential noise effects those that are institutional and non-residential.

THE MEASUREMENT AND IDENTIFICATION OF NOISE COSTS (CHAPTER 5)

One of the main problems in the analysis of noise is to find the distribution of the values that people place on various levels of noise. In the attribute model where there are only two levels of noise manifest in either homogeneous noisy or homogeneous quiet houses, there is only a limited amount of information that one can conceivably get from observed market behaviour. From the observed price differential between noisy and quiet houses we know only that those who buy quiet value it *at least* as much as the price they pay; but the market does not reveal how much. Similarly those who buy noisy houses must value the quiet *at less than* the price—but we do not know how much less. In principle one could find the distribution of people according to their taste for noise only by observing behaviour as we impose different quantities of noise and observe the reaction of people to the new conditions. One could calibrate the model by observing the fraction of movers under different conditions, and with sufficient observations one could sketch the distribution of people according to their revealed noise sensitivity. It is difficult, however, to obtain good information on movements of households.

When one turns from the attribute model to the more realistic model where householders can choose to buy any amount of quiet, the measurement difficulty largely disappears. In the long run the household's valuation of quiet is revealed by the amount it chooses to spend on quiet at the going price. For an (absolute) unit price elasticity of demand for quiet and any given level of income the fraction of income spent on quiet measures the household's taste for quiet. Thus we can adduce the distribution of people with respect to their tastes for a peaceful life. In principle, for a given NNI or CNR the house price depreciation will measure the taste for quiet of *all* households in that category; one would expect that in practice, however, there would be considerable variation about that mean value because of the mistakes that are made and because of all other factors that induce people to buy or stay.

The identification and measurement of the householder's surplus in his house poses a number of difficulties. It is rarely possible to observe situations where the prices of a certain number of houses are changed while the normal supply of other houses continues to be available at current market price. Experiments are never possible with people's property. It is relatively easy to calculate a maximum value for the distribution of the surplus from information about the price elasticity of demand for housing generally. Below that maximum the main source of data is surveys of householders. For what they are worth the answers of householders do appear to give results only a little below the maximum set by the general price elasticity of demand. One suspects, however, that from the methodology of such studies, there may be an upward bias.

Identification of the noise depreciation of houses is made relatively easy by the fact that the geographical noise shadow of runways is usually shaped like a dog's bone, whereas access characteristics are normally concentric. Consequently it is possible to observe houses with similar access characteristics but with different noise levels. It would be wrong, however, to give the impression that data on noise depreciation are easy to acquire; they are not.

Chapter 5 concludes with a technical note on the joint density distribution of the variables entering into the noise cost dynamics. In fact little is known about the joint density distribution and often 'reasonable' assumptions must be used instead of factual knowledge. But some of the correlations are known and are here illustrated.

EMPIRICAL EVIDENCE (CHAPTER 6)

The theoretical predictions of the first five chapters are examined in the light of empirical evidence. No new data have been collected for this study, although some new information which was collected for the London Roskill inquiry is reported. The various studies made of the noise depreciation of property (for a standard $25,000 house) in the United States all give broadly similar results—there is a 1 per cent depreciation in the value of a house for an increase of one unit CNR or a 0·7 per cent depreciation for one unit NNI. This result is the more remarkable since these studies, restricted to the jet age, covered quite different communities in different areas of the United States and used dissimilar methodologies. The data for London give somewhat higher noise depreciation for the same value of house (about 1·0 per cent per NNI), and one may find sensible rationalizations for such a higher value. Although one study by itself can be thought to contain little convincing substantive evidence, the accumulation of similar results lends verisimilitude to what would otherwise be unconvincing individual figures. Even more remarkable, the evidence suggests that NNI or CNR may be used as a *cardinal* measure for the quantity of noise over the relevant range of values, although naturally this is a very tentative result and will need many more tests to provide a very firm basis for policy. But provisionally we may say that for a given income and price of house, the market prices a movement from 40 to 45 NNI at the same rate as a movement from 45 to 50.

Evidence is also adduced to show that the elasticity of demand for quiet with respect to permanent income is in the region of 1·7 to 2·0. Such a high figure has been derived entirely from British data but one may well conjecture from other information that quiet is widely to be regarded as a luxury good. (Incidentially it is also consistent with the view that noise does not much matter in poor countries.) A high income elasticity of demand implies that there will be a trend increase in the demand for quiet as income *per capita* grows (at some 3 per cent per annum income growth, the demand for quiet will increase at annual rate 5–6 per cent). If there is no increase in the supply of quiet—and we shall argue in chapter 6 that such an increase in quiet from aircraft is unlikely to appear for some years—the increase in demand will manifest itself through an increase in the relative price of quiet. This is an important forecast since it drastically affects the evaluation of present policy decisions.[5] Clearly it would be much more satisfactory if the elasticity obtained from cross-section data were also checked against time series data—but no such data are at present available.

We explored methods of testing the proposition that the price elasticity of demand for quiet is (minus) unity. One such test would be to observe two separate communities broadly similar in composition and income levels where the relative supply of quiet differed considerably; then if the two communities spent the same amount on quiet we would have some evidence that the elasticity was about unity. Similarly if we had time series data on the fraction of income spent on quiet over time both for individual households and in aggregate we could also examine the changes (if any) in these fractions and so adduce evidence of the implied elasticity—although we would clearly have difficulty in sorting out the confounded effects of increases in *per capita* incomes and changes in the relative price of quiet. Unfortunately no such tests can be yet devised.

One of the other interesting features of the models discussed above is the fact that they predict *movement rates*—in particular they predict that when a new noise source is imposed there will be movements according to the 'moving rule' expressed above. Unfortunately, the research that provides most of the data on turnover rates had other purposes in mind, and the statistics

---

[5] In terms of the formal model it implies that the taste-for-quiet coefficient b_i is a function of income y—a doubling of income will increase b_i fourfold.

are not well adapted to our purposes. But a review of the evidence suggests that within the noisy areas the turnover of property rises some 25–50 per cent above normal. This rate is not dramatically inconsistent with the values forecast by our noise models—but is should be emphasized that such conformity does not in any way constitute a critical test of the noise model. The data are too fragmentary and fallible to be so construed.

Yet the message of this chapter is that it *is* possible to measure the amount which people do pay for a quiet life. With all the many qualifications put forward it seems to me that the evidence does provide a basis for a market valuation of noise.

POLICY (CHAPTER 7)

Granted the validity of the valuation of noise, the problem is to do something about it. There are two broad approaches to be pursued, which we may call the 'price approach' and the 'authorities approach'. With the price approach the objective is to ensure that those who generate the noise costs also pay for them. Furthermore, those who are injuriously affected by the noise should receive compensation. The objective is to create a sort of 'proprietary right' to environmental quiet. On the other hand with the authorities approach there is no attempt to reflect the value of noise in private accounts; decisions are made by the authorities about how noisy aircraft should be, where they should be allowed to fly, and who, if anyone, should be allowed to live in noisy areas. The planners and the politicians determine who shall or shall not suffer noise, whether I can fly at night, and so on.

Clearly the valuations adduced for environmental quiet must be used in formulating the price approach to policy. They are also very useful for any governmental body or planners who are anxious to formulate a rational policy for noise abatement and airport planning, since such valuations would indicate roughly how far they should go.

The authorities method has been the one normally adopted in airports and in airline controls. In part this has been due to the absence of any widely accepted valuation of noise, but there has also been a conviction that it would be administratively difficult to price noise and to compensate householders. Nevertheless, the price approach should be explored more intensively since it avoids the obvious loss of freedom and of efficiency of the authorities approach.

Airport landing fees could be arranged so that they reflect the relative noise costs of different types of aircraft. At present landing fees do vary according to the gross weight of the aircraft—and this factor has an important effect on the amount of noise produced—but they do not differentiate according to the number of people affected by noise, nor do they take account of the intensiveness of the use of the approach or take-off path. Finally, they do not discriminate between the quiet RB211 type of engine and the noisy turbo-jets. The case for a full scale revision of airport charging practices is strong—and the occasion should be used in order to vary such charges according to the noise costs.

See Page 128

Compensation for noise annoyance is often thought to be the appropriate way of reimbursing the expropriated owner for his loss of quiet. Theoretically the case for perfect compensation is powerful and difficult to assail. In practice, however, the basis for any such compensation is difficult to define and extremely difficult to implement. Compensation must depend on observed market valuations, and these change over time according to knowledge about the expected future conditions—including of course the amount of compensation. The circle is closed. The distribution of knowledge is such that some, and perhaps a large fraction, of the compensation will find its way into the pockets of those who have 'inside knowledge'. The case for compensating owners around *existing* sources of noise, however, is not strong since the capitalization of noise has long ago been incorporated into property values. The case for compensating owners for a new noise source is more reasonable. The compensation should be based on a simple rule. It is estimated that for a typical new airport affecting some 20,000 families the cost of such compensation would amount to $72 (£30 million) million—but again this is a very rough figure.

It is naturally tempting to use the figures on house depreciation due to noise to calculate the 'cost' in terms of the gross depreciation of property of an air transport movement. The figure for Heathrow-type conditions comes to about

£170 or \$430—probably of the order of £2 (\$5·00) per passenger. Such a value will vary considerably according to the conditions—such as the number of households affected, etc. One particular factor which will affect the noise rating considerably and so the value of noise nuisance is the size of the airport measured in terms of the number of air movements along the flight paths.

There are considerable economies of scale in making aircraft noise. The normal prescription therefore would be to concentrate noise at one place rather than spread it around thinly. To eliminate all aircraft noise is worth much more than 100 times the value of reducing flights by 1·0 per cent. One large busy airport is much better than six lightly used ones. This policy proposal then runs against the reactions of authorities to the pressures of noise lobbies. They are normally in favour of 'sharing the burden' among the different communities; but for a *local* noise group it is perfectly consistent with their interests to attempt to reduce the noise that they suffer even though the diversion of aircraft would generate ten times the annoyance elsewhere. The achievement of the aims of each local pressure group will make things worse for the community as a whole.

Zoning is the usual way of attempting to develop noise-compatible uses when a new noise source is imposed. Yet the evidence suggests that many people are willing to live in apparently noisy areas if the offsetting benefits such as accesibility are sufficiently large. It is difficult to see why the authorsities should not permit those who are relatively imperturbable from reaping the benefits of accessibility at small noise-disbenefit to themselves. To do so would be to throw away the valuable resource of accessible house sites. More planning powers and more vigorous enforcement of zoning regulations does not seem to be a suitable way of dealing with aircraft noise.

Acquisition of noise-affected property by the airport authority, to internalize the noise costs as well as the appreciation due to the greater case of access, is an expensive way of overcoming the noise problem. Indeed the expense is clearly prohibitive with existing airports. With new 'green field' airports, however, such an approach is feasible (as at Saint Scholastique in Quebec), but it does not necessarily mean that it is desirable.

The main objection is that such an expanded airport authority would have immense power—and such power would be concentrated in an activity where public corporations or departments of government have hitherto been very inefficient compared with private owners. The omens are not good.

The calculation of the noise costs of new airport sites is complicated by the need to calculate movement rates and the costs of airport noise in all future years. The noise model was developed to evaluate all these various factors and find the total costs—including movement costs and surpluses forgone—of noise. The application of this model to the sites at the Roskill inquiry into London's third airport gave useful 'benchmark' figures with which one may test simpler approaches. It is possible to derive a measure of the cost per household-NNI unit by knowing the variance of the distribution of households with respect to the NNI that they suffer. This figure can then be applied to the data for a new 'green fields' airport to get a measure in money terms of the noise nuisance that would be imposed on the existing houses. To this figure must be added the noise costs imposed on such institutions as hospitals, schools, and other establishments.

The model has not been adapted for answering questions about reductions in or the elimination of aircraft noise. However, one can clearly see that the benefits to be derived from reducing noise are considerably less than the costs which would be imposed by increasing noise by the same amount on a population of the same size. Nevertheless, the gross depreciation of households due to noise can be used as a high *upper* limit to the value of reducing noise on a community. We can use this measure in order to examine whether it would or would not be worth-while to quieten the existing fleet of jets by "retrofitting" their engines. Gross depreciation is clearly an overestimate of the benefits to be acquired by retrofitting the existing fleet of jets. Yet it is of interest to observe that if the costs of retrofit are taken to be $2 billion (£800 million), the gross appreciation of the houses so affected would probably be of the order of $1·4 billion (£550 million). So we conclude that from these data there is clearly no overwhelming case for requiring retrofit—but there is a case for a more refined investigation along these lines.

Finally, we might investigate the advantages of closing down Heathrow. We must allow for the fact that the residents have adapted to the noise—the perturbables have moved out and the insensitive residents have moved in. We conjecture—and it is no more than that—that the closing down of London Heathrow in 10 years' time would give rise to benefits at that date around £100 million. Such questions are, however, rather academic at present.

THE PRESENT STATE OF THE ECONOMICS OF NOISE

The theoretical analysis of the pricing of aircraft noise is straightforward and traditional and owes its origins to the incisive discussions of Alfred Marshall and the neo-classical economists. The concept of an *implicit* price is also as old as economics itself. The real difficulties are empirical ones that arise from the fact that there is no transaction which we can observe where a quantity of noise is exchanged against money. The noise transaction is tied in with the house transaction. We therefore have to adduce a quantitative measure of noise analogous to the quantity measure used for ordinary commodities. We have suggested that the NNI or CNR does appear to be a good quantitative measure in the economic sense that people pay the same price per unit. But the evidence on which such a view is held may well be thought to be quite flimsy. More evidence is required.

The empiciral evidence shows that there was a certain universality in the values derived. This is remarkable and rather surprising. If such consistency continues to prevail it will be extremely useful to have such simple laws to apply readily to new situations wherever they may occur. (The findings about elasticity, however, have only the London material to support them and no such claim for universality may be made.)

The analysis of policy proposals is in its infancy, and it is here where the authorities feel the pressure of the noise lobbies and the public. There is little doubt that much can be done to get the pricing of aircraft operations to reflect the costs or disbenefits that are imposed. The practical implementation of such principles would need to be carefully worked out but no

insurmountable administrative difficulties should be encountered. This is not the case with compensation proposals. Indeed
it is difficult to see how any widely applicable compensation
scheme could equitably work; and it is a great challenge for the
economist to produce a theory of compensation that is of some
practical use.

The theory and such empirical tests as have been carried out
do suggest that the economic analysis of noise could be usefully
applied in measuring the benefits and costs of noise reduction
and in deciding on the cost/benefit balance of new airports. Of
course decisions about retrofit and airport locations will be
made by politicians with votes as the currency; but it is important to know the objective evidence in order to be able to estimate what the costs are.

CHAPTER 2

The Measurement of Noise Nuisance

ECONOMIC AND ACOUSTICAL MEASURES OF NOISE

THERE is a natural quantitative measure of noise used by physicists. It is the energy content of a noise emission. But such a measure cannot be used as a simple measure of the human perception of noise nuisance. It is well known that certain types of noise such as high-frequency intermittent noise are much more annoying than a continuous low-pitched hum. Although simple physical measures of energy are not entirely useless, we must clearly search elsewhere for an appropriate measure of the human reaction to noise.

The real difficulty is that, unlike most goods and services, noise nuisance is not sold on the market. We cannot observe contracts being agreed for certain "quantities" of noise (except perhaps for concert halls or opera houses). There are no market data which can be used to identify homogeneous units of noise which sell for a given market price.

The absence of an explicit market for noise nuisance means that one must fabricate a measure from other data. Broadly speaking, two approaches are possible. First, one may try to find an *implicit* market and to measure noise in such a way that the price per unit of noise is constant—at least over a certain specified relevant range. I believe that this is the preferred approach since it corresponds most closely to the economic concept of quantity. A second approach is to find some composite measure of noise which corresponds monotonically with people's reactions to noise. Such reactions may emerge from psychological and sociological surveys of the affected areas. This second technique has been the approach adopted more or less universally with respect to aircraft noise nuisance. Virtually all measures of noise nuisance were devised along these lines.

There is a crucial difference between the economic or implicit-market measure of noise and the psycho-sociological survey measure. The implicit-market measure automatically defines units of measurement of noise which have the property of cardinality. In principle since all units command the same price on the (implicit) market they are equivalent. All cost the same. The units may vary in physical description, like different-sized bags of red and white potatoes, but for the economic analysis of noise we may take them as identical. In fact such an implicit-market measure should enable one to find the trade-off between noise intensity and number of occasions on which the noise is heard, just as the market permits one to find the trade-off between the colour and weight of potatoes.

There is no reason, however, why the functional form of any noise index should have these characteristics. The only strict requirement of a noise index is that it should exhibit ordinal properties so that as the noise nuisance increases the index measure increases. We cannot attribute any inherent cardinality to noise nuisance as such—so we cannot say "situation X is twice as noisy as situation Y", but only that "X is noisier than Y". However, although the efforts of acoustical research are concentrated on the formulation of an accurate ordinal measure, there does seem to be an attempt to measure noise nuisance in units that have approximately the same importance or meaning over the relevant range. Thus the aim is to develop an index so that moving the noise index from 40 to 45 is approximately the same as moving it from 45 to 50. In the social surveys the meaning of the "same" is the similarity of the intensity of human response—perhaps supported by objective evidence such as the fraction of complaints received or in the United States the number of law-suits started. If the noise-nuisance measure were calibrated against the number of complaints and from the psycho-sociological survey data and if the scale were skilfully chosen to be arithmetically equivalent, then one would expect that the noise-nuisance measure would nicely correspond with the data on implicit-market valuation—so that one unit of Noise Number Index or Composite Noise Rating would elicit the same price on the market whether it was added in a very noisy area or a moderately noisy area. One could then regard these noise-nuisance units as homogeneous.

It may strike the readers as extraordinarily fortuitous if such a correspondence were to be revealed in the evidence. But such seems to be the case. And we shall have occasion to demonstrate it, albeit very tentatively, in the empirical evidence in chapter 6. It is also a remarkable testimony to the sense and judgement of those who carried out the surveys and calibrated the indexes of noise nuisance. We now examine some measures of noise nuisance from these survey results.

COMPOSITE NOISE AND NUMBER MEASURES

Noise nuisance depends on the duration, the loudness and the mixture of tones (frequencies), and the number of times such noise is heard. The normal measure of loudness is the perceived noise decibel (PndB). This measures the loudness of aircraft noise but gives greater weight to the high-frequency tones— such as the high-pitched screech of turbo-jet engines—to which the human ear is most distressingly sensitive.[1] This PndB measure is the one that is used more or less universally in order to measure the loudness in terms of human experience.

In order to combine the loudness measure with an indication of the number of times the noise is experienced an index is formed of the following general class:

$$\text{Index} = \overline{(\text{PndB})} + k \log N - a,$$

where k and a are constants and N is a measure of the number of aircraft heard (in the U.K. on a summer day) and $\overline{\text{PndB}}$ is the average peak noisiness of aircraft. The measure $\overline{\text{PndB}}$ is obtained by finding the average of the energy intensities that produce the individual peaks—and this clearly exceeds the arithmetic average.

The *Noise Number Index* (NNI) is one that has been much used in the United Kingdom and is found by writing $k = 15$ and $a = 80$, so that:

$$(\text{NNI}) = \overline{(\text{PndB})} + 15 \log N - 80.$$

The NNI was derived from a social survey by McKennell in the London (Heathrow) area.[2] A sample of people were classified according to district by the noisiness and number of aircraft and these measures were correlated with the subjective reactions as measured by 58 socio-psychological variables. The

[1] See Kryter (1959), p. 1415.
[2] See Wilson Committee, (1963).

NNI formula was thought to give the best fit to the data.[3] New evidence collected in a new social survey in 1967 suggests that the NNI places too much emphasis on the number of aircraft and not sufficient on their loudness.[4] An amendment allowing for such a criticism would bring the index nearer to its rivals, the CNR and Indice Isopsophique, and would deal with some of the criticisms that have been levelled against it.[5]

Perhaps the most serious charge against the NNI is that it does not allow for any method of dealing with differential fractions of night and daytime noise. The NNI was calibrated around Heathrow during the period of 1961 and consequently reflects the relative fraction of night noise at that time. The Roskill Commission, while emphasizing that there was very little evidence, accepted the view that one should add 10 NNI points for equivalent night noise and emphasize especially the peak noise value.[6]

The value for the constant a was chosen so that if the first two terms added to 80 the NNI would be zero. It is widely argued that noise nuisance exists whenever a PndB in excess of 75 PndB occurs; and it might be represented that the ambient noise level in the Heathrow area is of the order of 62 PndB on the average. Thus it is difficult to settle on any natural zero rating for the NNI. As we shall see from the data on noise depreciation of houses in the Heathrow and Gatwick areas the zero line is approximately 30–35 NNI. Below 30 NNI there is no evidence of any depreciation due to noise.

The *Composite Noise Rating* (CNR) is widely used in the United States and is formed as follows:

$$(\text{CNR}) = \overline{(\text{PndB})} + 10 \log N - 12.$$

Some corrections are made to the peak noise figure for night

[3] It must be noted, however, that Galloway and Bishop (1970) fitted the CNR to the London data and claim to have obtained with $k = 10$ rather than $k = 15$ "as statistically significant a fit to the annoyance data ... and provides a considerably more palatable physical description of noise exposure".

[4] These results were published in 1972. It seems, however, that the 1967 survey was poorly planned and did not even have a "control group" against which the positive results could be calibrated. See Noise Advisory Council (1972).

[5] For example, see the criticism in Galloway and Bishop (1970). See also P. E. Hart (1973), pp. 137–51.

[6] Roskill Report, pp. 60–1, §§ 7.17–7.22.

and daytime operations and an adjustment is made for the
duration of the noise. This formula was obtained from a study
of complaints around various civil and military airports. It is
very similar in form to the NNI. Over the relevant range of
NNI (30–60) and CNR (98–118) it can be assumed as a good
approximation that:

one unit CNR = one and a half units NNI;

one unit NNI = two-thirds of a unit CNR.

TABLE 2.1

NNI reactions

NNI (refers to daytime 0600–1800 hours except where stated)	Social survey around Heathrow (for Wilson Committee 1963)
8	Average reaction, "not at all annoyed by aircraft noise"
32	Average reaction, "a little annoyed by aircraft noise"
35 (night)	
40	
42	Average reaction, "moderately annoyed by aircraft noise"
45 (night)	
50	
60	Average reaction, "very much annoyed by aircraft noise"

Source: Wilson committee (1963).

The *Isopsophic Index* (or Indice Isopsophique) is used in
France and is obtained from the following formula:

$$(\text{II}) = (\overline{\text{PndB}}) + 10 \log N - 30.$$

3

Thus its basic form is the same as that of the NNI and the CNR. However, night operations are treated in a more complex way. Peak noises and numbers from 2000 hours to 0200 hours receive three times the weight of those in the remainder of the night hours. The reasoning for this weight emerged from a social survey of Orly, Le Bourget, Marseilles, and Lyons.

The *Störindex* ($\bar{Q}$) is used by the Federal Republic of Germany and is expressed in the formula:

$$\bar{Q} = 13 \cdot 3 \log \left(\frac{1}{T} \int_0^T 10^{L_A(t)/13 \cdot 3} \, dt \right),$$

where L is the sound level in PndB. This form and the particular constants used appear to be derived from psycho-acoustic experiments. Since this index considers the duration of noise as an explicit argument of the function one cannot make direct comparisons between it and the CNR or NNI.

The *Noise Exposure Forecast* (NEF) is the most recent attempt to introduce a more sophisticated measure which takes into account in a more satisfactory way the relative incidence and effects of night noise. The basis of the index is the aircraft operation, either landing or take-off, along a particular flight path. Thus for aircraft i on flight path j, we have the element:

$$\mathrm{NEF}(ij) = \mathrm{EPN}(ij) + 10 \left\{ \log \frac{N(\mathrm{day})(ij)}{K(\mathrm{day})} + \frac{N(\mathrm{night})(ij)}{K(\mathrm{night})} \right\} - C,$$

where

$\mathrm{NEF}(ij)$ = Noise Exposure Forecast value of aircraft class i along flight path j;

$\mathrm{EPNL}(ij)$ = Effective perceived noise level produced at the given point by aircraft class i on path j;

N is number of aircraft per 15 hour day or 9 hour night; K are normalizing constants, chosen so that when $N(\mathrm{day}) = 20$ there is no addition for number, i.e. if $N(\mathrm{day}) = 20$, $K(\mathrm{day}) = 20$, so that the first term in the curled bracket is zero;

$K(\mathrm{night})$ is chosen so that for the same average number of flights per hour during day or night the NEF contribution for night would be 10 units higher than for day, i.e.

$$\frac{\log K(\mathrm{night})}{9} = \frac{\log K(\mathrm{day})}{15}, \quad \text{i.e. } K(\mathrm{night}) = 1 \cdot 2$$

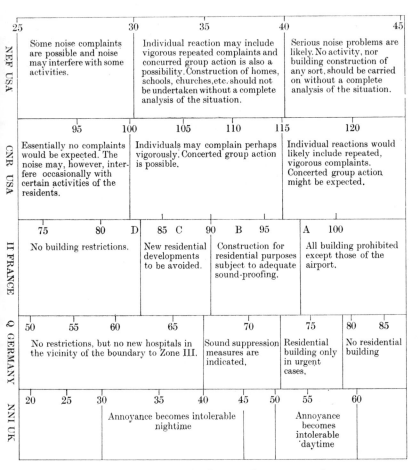

Fig. 2.1. Approximate equivalences between noise exposure indices and response or land use descriptions. Source: Galloway and Bishop (1970).

This standardizing process therefore gives considerably more weight to night noise in the ratio 20 to 1·2 or 16·7 to 1. C is chosen as an arbitrary normalizing constant (88). The total NEF is then calculated by summing the individual NEFs as exponents of 10 and then taking the logarithm:

$$\text{NEF} = 10 \log \sum_{ij} 10^{\frac{1}{10}\{\text{NEF}(ij)\}}.$$

Undoubtedly the NEF is more sophisticated than the CNR or NNI measures which it is intended to replace. But the NEF is more costly to calculate since it requires EPNL noise measures rather than the PNL (or PndB) measures used in CNR and NNI. And as far as one can discover the NEF has not yet been calibrated with respect to socio-psychological measures such as the survey of McKennell for the Wilson Committee on Noise (1963). Nevertheless, the NEF has distinct advantages over earlier measures and may well ultimately replace them.

EQUIVALENCE OF NOISE INDICES

As is clear from the discussion of the various measures there is a close correspondence between them (Figure 2.1). However, the variations in the treatment of numbers as against loudness, and of night noise as against day noise mean that there can be no precise rules for transforming one index into another. For example, the differential effects of the number of aircraft can be seen in the spread of the lines of Figure 2.2 for the four indices there considered. The CNR and Indice Isopsophique (II) are similar and the $\bar{Q}$ and NNI are also similar but allow the numbers of aircraft to have a larger influence.

It is very useful to have transformation scales and these have been calculated—as approximate values—by Galloway and Bishop (1970, p. 48). The following approximate transforms will be used in this study:

Unit change NEF = 1·5 unit change CNR = 2·25 unit change NNI;

Unit change CNR = 1·5 unit change NNI;

Unit change NNI = 0·67 unit change CNR.

It will be observed that all the indices move in the same arithmetical way—it is simply the units and the origin that differs. Thus approximately one may take it that all the indices are linear transforms with a more or less arbitrary zero and an arbitrary scale of measurement.[7]

---

[7] In my view attempts to eliminate the arbitrariness from the zero by imagining a state of "perfect peace" or perhaps "normal peace" have been unsuccessful, as, perhaps, one might well expect. However, if one accepts the assumption that the true or economically meaningful measure of noise is simply a linear transform of the NNI or CNR or NEF, then an effective zero can be found. Evidence on this issue is discussed in chapter 6.

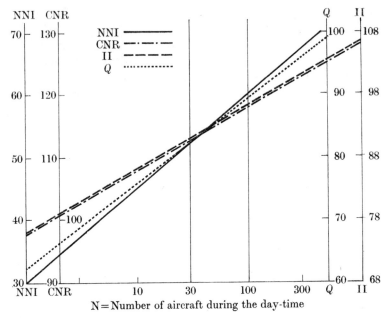

FIG. 2.2. Differential Effects of the Number of Aircraft on the Four
Indices. Source: Roskill Commission (1970a).

PUBLIC ACCEPTANCE OF THE VALIDITY OF
NOISE INDICES

Notwithstanding the intensive research of acoustical scientists and statisticians one of the acid tests of any noise measure
is its acceptability. Many criticisms were aimed at the Noise
Number Index and related measures during the hearings
(Stage V) of the Roskill Commission. First it was argued that
the NNI was not appropriate for measuring the effect of noise on
activities dependent on intelligibility of speech. The noisiness of
individual aircraft then must be considered because this
determines the degree of interference with speech. Secondly, it
is clear that people will vary according to their reactions to any
given mix of peak noise and frequency.

In spite of all the various particular objections to any
measure such as NNI there was wide agreement during the
course of the Roskill hearings that no better and comprehen-
sible measure could be devised. The small improvements

which appeared later in the NEF measure would undoubtedly have been welcome, however, since they do take account explicitly of the variation in the night noise component. But it is clear that all the indices can be used sensibly and efficiently provided that the user bears in mind precisely what is being measured. Then one will normally claim no more for the measure than it can deliver.

Later, in chapter 7, we shall suggest simple compensation criteria based on these noise measures. Whether the public would accept such measures is another story which has yet to be told.

CHAPTER 3

The Household Demand for Quiet

IMPLICIT PRICES AND QUANTITY

IN economic analysis one normally is concerned with the concepts of quantity and price. For the individual family or household, which is the concern of this chapter, the price can be taken as given and the family adjusts the quantity it purchases to conform to its tastes. The price and quantity magnitudes are observed as the characteristic features of contracts entered into on the market—so much quantity at such-and-such a price. The phenomenon of 'residential quiet', however, clearly does not have these characteristics. As we noted in chapter 2, there is no market on which one can observe people making explicit contracts for so much residential quiet at a specified price. The acquisition of residential quiet is a by-product of the contractual arrangements of purchasing a property.

But house sale contracts do not specify that the right to a specified degree of residential quiet is also transferred along with the real property. No right of this kind is recognised contractually. What the purchaser buys is the *probability* of residential quiet; he takes his chances, making his own judgements and, of course, paying the penalty if he is careless or unlucky. In this respect residential quiet is similar to many other amenity features of houses—such as the view. In principle one should analyse the economics of noise in terms of these probabilities. But since they do not play any central role in theory or policy we shall usually assume that, although not contractually guaranteed, the buyer knows with certainty the degree of residential quiet he is buying.[1]

The purchase of residential quiet is therefore an *implicit* transaction. By comparing the price of houses which are noisy

---

[1] The issue of imperfect information is taken up again in the policy discussion.

with the price of houses that are quiet we can discover how much is spent on securing residential quiet. However, this comparison gives us only the *expenditure* on quiet; it does not tell us either the quantity or the price. In order to derive the price some measure of quantity must be adduced or assumed.

One approach that has been much used for analytical purposes is to assume that houses are either noisy or quiet; residential quiet is then an attribute not a quantity.[2] The price of residential quiet is then identically equal to the expenditure. Such an assumption is analytically convenient and we shall use it extensively in the following pages. It disposes of the problem of measuring the quantity of noise by assuming it away. Unfortunately the assumption also obscures many of the interesting features of the householder's decision—we cannot analyse for example why A prefers to buy a really quiet house while B prefers only a moderately quiet one. This is a serious and indeed crucial disability for many applications, so we must devise another method of analysis.

The second approach therefore is to attempt to adduce *some measure of noisiness that has economic validity*. The characteristic feature about normal markets is that the price per unit of a commodity is the same; equally the units in which noisiness or quiet is measured must have the same price. Thus the expenditure and the quantity should increase proportionately (or at least linearly if we allow an arbitrary quantity origin in the measurement of noise nuisance) when we observe people buying residential quiet at the same time in the same market. Then the price of quiet may be taken to be the same over the cross-section. The definition of an appropriate unit of quantity is an empirical matter and will be discussed at length in chapter 6. We merely note at this stage that the standard measures of noise reviewed in chapter 2 turns out to be reasonably acceptable quantity units over the relevant range.

This second approach, which assumes that on the market a householder can buy any amount of quiet at the ruling price, is the basic assumption which we adopt throughout this chapter. But the fact that the purchase of quiet is 'tied' to the purchase

---

[2] Using this assumption S. Plowden, M. Paul, and J. Wise have all pursued the analytical fine points of the economics of noise. See Roskill Commission (1970b), days 47–70.

of a house does give rise to a number of special problems—
especially in the process of adjustment from one set of circumstances to another.

THE DEMAND FOR QUIET

For the individual or the family therefore it is a convenient
first approximation to treat residential quiet as a "good" that
can be bought on the free market. When one buys a house for a
residence one purchases a package of more or less desirable
features such as a pleasing aspect, convenient layout, etc. One
also buys a certain quantity of residential quiet. Let us suppose
that there is a sufficient supply of houses for the market to be
competitive and that there are many potential buyers and
sellers for each house with its associated residential quiet. No
one buyer or seller can have any appreciable effect on the price.
Secondly, we make the important assumption that search and
transactions costs are zero. This assumption, characteristic of
all standard economics, is analogous to the no-friction assumption of classical mechanics. It is so demonstrably at variance
with the facts that it may well seem absurd to make it. And in
the empirical work one must reject the assumption, and integrate search and moving costs explicitly into the analysis.
But as in the physical analogue of the laws of motion, we can
make much progress by first assuming that there are no
search and moving costs, and then when the basic notions are
clear such costs can be grafted on to the results.

In principle, therefore, the individual or family faces a fixed
price for residential quiet and so costlessly adjusts the quantity
purchased according to taste. Another interesting problem is
whether or not residential and other quiet is a superior good.
Holding the price of quiet constant and increasing permanent
income, one would regard it as a luxury good if people spent a
larger fraction of their income in buying quiet. This implies
that people are then substituting quiet for other goods as the
level of income increases. A casual review of the evidence does
suggest that this is the case, but we pursue this subject with
empirical evidence in chapter 6.

One might also examine various archetypes of the demand
for quiet using the traditional approaches of indifference
curves. Suppose, for example, there are those who are quite

imperturbable with respect to aircraft noise—then we can describe their indifference curve as A in Figure 3.1. They will not be prepared to give up any income in order to buy quiet. B, on the other hand, describes the indifference curve of a man who has the same income Y_A when all is bedlam (quiet = 0) but who would be prepared to give up other goods to get peace.

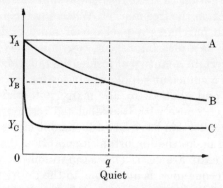

FIG. 3.1. Indifference curves of income and quiet.

In fact we may suppose that, at a given price for quiet, B would buy q of quiet and retain Y_B of his income. C describes another extreme case; this sensitive person is willing to buy peace at any price provided he has a subsistence income left.[3]

From the indifference curves one can generate a household demand curve for residential quiet—as the price is varied so the quantity purchased will change. With the usual assumptions the curve will be downward sloping. The individual can take all other prices as given since he is such a small fraction of the total market. So a fall in the price of quiet (all other prices fixed) will result in him being better off and buying more quiet, provided that quiet is not a Giffen good.[4]

---

[3] We may use this figure to note the consequences of imposing certain fixed standards of quite. Suppose q is imposed as the standard of quiet in the whole community, which had hitherto suffered bedlam (quiet = 0), then it is clear that the valuation of the q regulation by A, B, and C will differ. Thus if the total community were to consist of equal numbers of A, B, and C we might compare then the sum $\frac{1}{3}\{0 + (Y_A Y_B) + (Y_A Y_{sub})\}$ as the average amount the consumer would be willing to pay for the regulation.

[4] In chapter 6 we shall show that the evidence suggests that quiet is a "luxury"; as incomes increase people spend a larger fraction of their income on a quiet life.

Now consider a small reduction (Δp) in the price of quiet from p to ($p - \Delta p$) all other prices and income fixed. Then we can calculate the increase in valuation as a consequence. First, we note that the increase in income is clearly equal to the quantity bought multiplied by the observed fall in price, i.e. $q \, \Delta p$. (We can ignore the change $\frac{1}{2}(\Delta p \, \Delta q)$ since it is of the second order of smalls.) The income gain is approximately $q \, \Delta p$, and the utility gain is $\lambda q \, \Delta p$ where λ is the marginal utility of income. With a constant marginal utility of income we can represent the money value of the gain by the income gain $q \, \Delta p$ for small variations in price.[5]

It is clear also that such calculations can be carried out however many small price changes occur. But the rule is that we hold all other prices constant in order to calculate the gain from a given small price change. The order in which such calculations are made does not matter,[6] provided that the demand curves are Hicksian Compensated. In practice this means provided that the income effects are of the "second order of smalls". For example, if the price of quiet houses rises and the price of noisy houses falls, then we can either (1) hold the price of quiet houses at its original level and measure the effect of the fall in the noisy house price and then, holding the low price for noisy houses, measure the disutility of the higher price for quiet houses, or (2) hold the price of noisy houses at its original level and measure the disutility of the higher price of quiet houses and then for a fixed high price of quiet measure the advantage of having cheaper noisy houses.

Another well-known singular disadvantage of the monetary measure is the fact that the marginal utility of income might be thought to change as a consequence of changes in real income brought about by changes in price. There is no way around this difficulty except to argue that, for the changes envisaged, the variation in λ is small enough to be ignored. I suspect that as far as individual variations in real income and λ are concerned

[5] To establish these obvious results and to examine the case where the consumer also owns commodities (e.g. quiet houses) the reader is referred to the mathematical note at the end of this chapter.

[6] See mathematical note for a development of these points.

this is a sensible view for the purposes of examining the effects of aircraft noise. The important distinction, however, is *between families*. There may be a considerable variation between a rich man's and a poor man's λ. It is not sensible to aggregate money measures as indicators of utility. This is a problem which much exercised economists in their evidence by the Roskill Commission and we shall return to it later.[7]

QUIET, THE HOUSE-SALE TIE-IN, AND SURPLUSES

It is observed that the decision about residential quiet, although we have represented it as a continuous independent decision, can clearly not be so simply regarded in practice. To buy residential quiet one must buy or rent a house in the appropriate area. If "units" of houses were identical homogeneous small units and were on offer in every location then each person would have no difficulty in nicely adjusting the number of house units he purchased in the location which produced the desired degree of quiet at that price. We can simply buy the number of identical homogeneous units which are equally desirable.

But it is clear that even with no costs of selling moving and buying many persons normally would not sell if they were offered the market price of their house. They get used to living in a particular house and neighbourhood. They make adjustments so that the house is adapted to their peculiar needs and tastes. Any other house bought on the market with the money raised by the sale of an existing house would have to go through the adaptation period and would involve considerable disbursements of money and time. Similarly, people have friends in the neighbourhood and the children get used to the schools and playgrounds. All these factors give rise to an attachment to a particular house.

Such an attachment is reflected in the fact that although people may receive offers considerably above the market price, some will not sell, on the rationalization "I like it here." In order to analyse preferences of this kind it is convenient to construct a simple case and present the results in the form of demand curves. Let us suppose that there are two locations for houses A and B which are identical in the degree of quiet.

[7] Roskill Commission (1970b), days 1–15.

Consider now the demand curves of a particular potential owner for housing units either at A or at B; these demands are represented in Figure 3.2 by the curves labelled D_a and D_b respectively. Clearly location A is preferred to B and we might conveniently suppose that B is the next best alternative to the preferred location at A. Let us also imagine that the cost of buying additional units of house-room at both A and B is

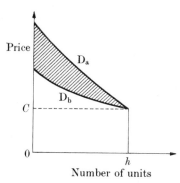

F IG. 3.2. Micro-demands for housing units.

constant at a unit value of C. Whether the potential owner buys at A or B he will clearly have an incentive to purchase additional house-room units if his marginal valuation exceeds the cost C. Suppose for simplicity that for both A and B this marginal condition gives rise to the same *quantity* of house-room at h for both A and B. Now let us consider the realistic all-or-nothing situation when the potential owner inhabits A— how much would he be prepared to pay rather than be evicted from house A and given the alternative of purchasing house B ? With zero movement cost and the same cost per unit the amount spent on house-room is the same; but he clearly values A more than B. The shaded area gives us an approximate value of the differential surplus value of A over B.[8]

We can also put the alternative question: how much would we have to pay in order to get the resident voluntarily to vacate his house at A and move to B ? This will be rather larger than

[8] In the Roskill Stage V hearings a concept called a consumer surplus was used. But the reader will observe that the Roskill measure really was differential surplus in the sense that is used here. The Roskill papers are not explicit on this point of interpretation.

the amount he would be willing to pay to stay where he is in A which we examined in the previous paragraph. I might require a very large sum indeed to induce me voluntarily to move; but if I were told that I were moving I would be prepared to pay out of my own pocket a smaller amount to stay put.

We can call these values respectively the high differential (HDS) and low differential surplus (LDS) respectively.[9] They can respond to the case first (LDS) when the house-owner has to say how much *he will pay* to recover a right taken away from him (to live in A), and secondly (HDS) when the householder is asked how much *he would need to be bribed* in order to move from A to B, i.e. voluntarily give up his right to live in A. In the HDS case where he receives the bribe one would expect that his demands for house-room would rise relative to the LDS case where he has to pay to stay where he is. In other words the LDS measures his *willingness-to-pay* to stay put whereas the HDS measures the *compensation* he would require voluntarily to move.

This argument is couched in terms of the "personalized advantages" of house A over other alternatives. But the same arguments can be used to examine the effects of noise. Suppose that a house-owner, at present occupying A, is suddenly and without warning subjected to noise that is expected to continue in perpetuity. Then clearly his valuation of the house at A will fall. It may not fall enough to make the quiet location at B preferable so he will stay in A. On the other hand, the noise may be so great that his valuation of A falls below B he will sell A and move to B. The loss is represented by the differential surplus in the curves for each case. The differential surplus between A-without-noise and A-with-noise represents the man's evaluation of the noise nuisance as far as residential quiet is concerned. This was called N in the Roskill *Proceedings* and *Report*. Thus if N exceeds the differential surplus (which Roskill called S) the man will move; while if N is less than S the man will stay and put up with noise in order to continue to enjoy those particular qualities of his house and neighbourhood.[10]

[9] The reader will note that we could have called this the "compensating" and "equivalent" consumer surplus but the application is somewhat different from the normal usage.

[10] Roskill Commission (1972a).

It is necessary to ask at this stage whether the HDS or the LDS is the appropriate basis for settling whether a man sells and moves or stays put. In practical applications of airport noise the issue is quite clear. The airport is constructed with flight paths over his house. No one asks the residents' permission and no one asks him how much we would be willing to accept to give up his peace. It is gone. He has to adjust to that fact. So it is clearly the LDS that is relevant for estimating movements due to noise. One might argue however, that in measuring the *cost* of noise to those who suffer, either by moving or by staying put, the HCS is appropriate. The HCS measures the compensation owners require to ensure that they are as well off as they were before the noise was imposed.[11] Whether there is any significant practical difference between the HCS and LCS is an issue that we take up later.

CHANGES IN PRICE AND THE NUMBER OF HOUSING UNITS BOUGHT

So far we have assumed that the price per unit of house-room remains constant whether it be noisy or quiet. This is clearly absurd and one must now ask what happens if the price of quiet houses rises and that of noisy houses falls. Figure 3.3 illustrates

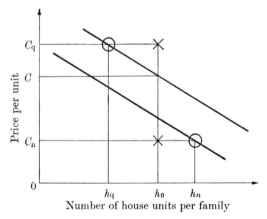

FIG. 3.3. Micro (family)-demand for housing units.

[11] Arguments along these lines, but not precisely the same, have been advanced by Margaret Paul (1971), p. 306. See also A. A. Walters (1972), p. 287.

the case of differing prices for noisy and quiet houses. Let us also make the assumption that there are only two kinds of homogeneous house-room units—noisy units and quiet units. Suppose, for simplicity, that the quantity of house units bought by each family is fixed at h_0 so that we begin with h_0 house units purchased by the family at the pre-airport price of C. The airport's noise causes the price of quiet houses to rise C_q and the price of noisy houses to fall C_n. Suppose that all families, of which the one shown in Figure 3.3 is representative, are owner-occupiers. Then those who remain quiet would enjoy an imputed income increase due to the capital gain $(C_q - C)h_0$. The owner could, however, sell his quiet house at the market price and buy a noisy house instead. The smaller the valuation of noise (N) for a fixed quantity of house-room (h_0) and the greater the difference between the price of quiet house (C_q) and that of a noisy house (C_n) the more likely that the owner of the quiet house will sell and move. A similar argument can be easily constructed for the owner of the noisy house.[12]

Thus if there is a fixed amount of house-room (h_0) per family we can find the moving rule. The household will move if the noise valuation exceeds the differential surplus less any capital loss incurred by so moving.

One particular difficulty of this (Roskill) approach is that "a house is a house"; no adaptation is envisaged, so quiet houses, now more valuable, are not sub-divided among more people. Noisy houses are not more sparsely occupied or left empty longer or allowed to deteriorate more. Similarly, there will be a long-term supply effect as higher-density building takes place in quiet areas, and so on. Although it is true in principle that something of this sort would occur, it is difficult to regard it as a serious criticism of the approach. Such effects cannot be quantitatively important and so it is best to leave these elaborations out of the model. They can be described in our Figure 3.3 above; instead of the equilibrium points being shown as the circles, the Roskill assumption supposes that the householders are constrained to choose between the crosses. Instead of buying larger noisy houses or small quiet houses, Roskill assumed that

---

[12] Note that we assume that there is no income effect (of the capital gain or loss) on this demand for house-room. This is for convenience only and the reader may add it in if he wishes.

no such adjustment occurred. One may well conjecture that such differences are of a trivial order in practical applications, and survey evidence does not suggest that there are noticeable signs of this adjustment.

THE MOVING RULE OF THE HOUSEHOLD

The last item to take into account at the micro-level is search and movement costs. These are not trivial and certainly cannot be ignored, as anyone who has had occasion to move house will well know. It is not perfectly clear that search and movement costs can be taken as a constant determined by factors exogenous to the individual. The investment of time and expense which one puts into house search should be a function of the expected pay-off, and this might be thought to vary with one's wage rate and perhaps proportionately with the price of houses—but one could adduce evidence against this. Nevertheless as a rough approximation we can take search and removal costs (R) as fixed for the individual so that the moving rule here becomes:

$$N > S + D + R - \text{move}$$
$$N < S + D + R - \text{stay put}$$

where N is the differential noise evaluation; S is the differential surplus (LDS); D is the capital *loss* due to the difference in prices; R is removal costs. This is the basic moving rule which should be used throughout the replications of the dynamic effects of adjustment to a new or more intensified source of noise.

One point of both interpretation and substance needs to be incorporated in this decision rule. In principle the rule applies at all moments of time. But the values N, S, R, and D must be understood as the *present values* of future expected outgoings or valuations of psychic costs discounted at some particular rate of time preference. Thus a sensitive person might move even though peace prevailed at present if he held firm expectations about future flight paths, and perhaps expected D to increase at some future date when the airport intensified operations, and so on.[13]

---

[13] A second point of trivial theoretical but considerable practical importance is concerned with the treatment of insulation costs. In principle we interpret the difference between A_q and A_n as excluding any net benefits (under A_n) that are derived from incurring expenditure on insulation. We assume that such spending has been optimized and treat all effects as net.

He would start searching for a new house as soon as his expectations were crystallized in order to give himself sufficient time to scan the market.

So far the analysis has been set out in terms of owner-occupiers. But most of the results can easily be adapted to fit the case of property that is rented. Obviously the costs of moving differ and capital gains mostly accrue to the landlords. The tenant does not incur the expense of selling and buying although he has a somewhat similar cost of searching for a new property. It seems therefore that with some distributional complications the landlord–tenant situation can easily be incorporated. Regulated tenancies and local authority housing cause more problems. Movement from such a house then must incur loss of the advantages of a regulated tenancy. In principle this can be treated as an additional movement cost. Such rigidities in the regulated housing sector do give rise to additional costs due to noise but it is very difficult to measure such a phenomenon. No observed costs can be adduced in evidence. In practice therefore such people are treated as though they were owner-occupiers, but we return to this in chapter 6.

This completes our discussion of the economics of noise pertaining to the family. The reader may object, however, that we have only covered house prices, and so we have only incorporated residential quiet in our analysis. This question of what is or is not comprehended by these valuations is taken up when we have discussed the market relationships and how prices respond to family behaviour patterns.

APPENDIX: A MATHEMATICAL NOTE ON UTILITY MAXIMIZATION AND DEMAND CURVES

1. Define the indirect utility function of an individual as utility maximized for a given vector of prices and a level of income (y) consuming q_j units of the jth commodity as

$$U(q_1, q_2, \ldots q_n)$$
$$= U\{q_1(p_1, p_2 \ldots p_n), q_2(p_1, p_2 \ldots p_n) \ldots \ldots\}$$
$$= U(p_1, p_2, p_3 \ldots p_n, y).$$

Income is comprised of fixed endowments of the n commodities $(i = 1, 2 \ldots n)$ which are denoted by $k_i(i = 1, \ldots n)$ and general lump sum spending power L. Thus

$$y = \sum_{i=1}^{n} p_i k_i + L.$$

The consumer then distributes his income among the n commodities buying $x_i(i = 1 \ldots n)$ of each.

2. Now consider how utility changes in response to a change in the price of the commodity. We examine:

$$\frac{\partial U}{\partial p_j} = \sum_{i=1}^{n} \left(\frac{\partial U}{\partial x_i} \frac{\partial x_i}{\partial p_j} + \frac{\partial U}{\partial y} \frac{\partial y}{\partial p_j} \right).$$

But in equilibrium

$$\frac{\partial U}{\partial x_i} = \lambda p_i, \quad \text{where} \quad \lambda = \frac{\partial U}{\partial y},$$

and

$$\frac{\partial y}{\partial p_j} = k_j, \quad \text{since} \quad y = \sum p_i k_i + L.$$

Also

$$\frac{\partial U}{\partial y} = \sum_{i=1}^{n} \frac{\partial U}{\partial x_i} \frac{\partial x_i}{\partial y}, \quad \text{and} \quad \sum p_i \frac{\partial x_i}{\partial y} = 1,$$

so that

$$\frac{\partial U}{\partial p_j} = \lambda \sum_{i=1}^{n} p_i \left(\frac{\partial x_i}{\partial p_j} + \frac{\partial x_i}{\partial y} \frac{\partial y}{\partial p_j} \right)$$

reduces to

$$\frac{\partial U}{\partial p_j} = \lambda (k_j - x_j),$$

which is economically obvious. When the price increases you will be better off if you are a net seller rather than a net buyer of the i commodity. Thus, in our context if I owned a quiet house and was myself imperturbable so that I rented a noisy house, then I would be better off if the price of quiet increased (since k_j would be much greater than x_j for me).

3. For simplicity let us suppose that there are no domestic capitalists—all houses are owned by foreign capitalists and rented to domestic tenants. Then $k_j = 0 (j = 1, 2 \ldots n)$ so that:

$$\frac{\partial U}{\partial p_j} = -\lambda x_j.$$

4. If we now examine the change in utility for a finite (not "small") change in the price p_i, we note that λ is a function of real income and in general cannot be presumed to remain fixed. If, however, we were to assume that the changes in λ as a consequence of the variations in p_i and so of real income were of a small order we could integrate the area under the conventional demand curve.

5. With more than one price changing—let us imagine two that prices change, p_i and p_j—then the generalization is straightforward. For we have:

$$\mathrm{d}U = \frac{\partial U}{\partial p_i}\,\mathrm{d}p_i + \frac{\partial U}{\partial p_j}\,\mathrm{d}p_j.$$

With the substitution above, we obtain

$$-\lambda^{-1}\,\mathrm{d}U = x_i(p_1, p_2, \ldots p_i, p_j \ldots y)\,\mathrm{d}p_i +$$
$$+ x_j(p_1, p_2, \ldots p_i, p_j \ldots y)\,\mathrm{d}p_j.$$

For a given finite change in prices p_i and p_j we integrate under the jth demand curve for a fixed price p_i, and then under the ith demand curve for a fixed price p_j.[14] The interest in this case is that normally a change in the market price of one commodity is accompanied by changes in other market prices as people switch their purchases and as supply adjusts. For *market* demand curves therefore the case of multiple price changes is the interesting one.

---

[14] Provided that $\partial x_i/\partial p_j = \partial x_j/\partial p_i$ it does not matter in which order we proceed to integrate. A sufficient condition is that the income effects be zero. In general this will be true for all compensated demand curves of the Hicksian kind.

CHAPTER 4

The Market for Housing and the Costs of Noise

MARKET VALUES AND THEIR MEANING

NOISE normally has an effect on the market price of houses and also on the rent which an owner may obtain for his property. The price of houses is determined by the stocks of houses at any moment of time and the demand for those stocks in the portfolios of asset-holders. But since many houses are owner-occupied the asset also provides the services of accommodation at an albeit implicit rent. The noisiness of the residence is one of the quality features of the asset. Provided that noise is always to be interpreted as a "bad" for all families in the community, one should expect a price differential between quiet and noisy property. If noisy and quiet houses were the same price every sensitive householder would choose the quiet house; thus the price of noisy houses would have to fall and price of quiet houses rise in order to clear the market for the existing stocks of the different types of houses.

However, a number of questions arise from such a situation. First, one may ask whether in fact there will always be such a differential. Clearly, the assumption that all people regard aircraft noise as a "bad" is not true. Some are deaf or insensitive and indeed some people positively enjoy noise. People vary considerably in their evaluation and tolerance of noise. Secondly, the differential between the prices of noisy and quiet houses must depend in some way on the relative number of houses in each category. Similarly the effects of a change in the relative numbers of noisy and quiet houses will depend on the percentage size of that change. Thirdly, as emphasized in chapters 2 and 3, noise is not an attribute but a continuum. People can buy as much noise (or quiet) as they like. We need to examine the effects of such a realistic interpretation of the noise measure on the price and quantity of noise. In particular the effects of different supplies of noise on price and expenditure need to be explored. Fourthly, we must also inquire in the dynamics of adjustment to changes in the fraction of noisy and quiet areas. In particular we must ask what are the effects of frictions in the system, such as the cost of searching and moving house and the "surplus" valuation over and above market price which most house-owners and tenants enjoy.

We begin first in section 2 with the "attribute" model where one can buy either a quiet or a noisy house. One cannot buy a nicely adjusted quantity of quiet. Later we examine a simple model where such adjustments are possible.

A SIMPLE SUPPLY–DEMAND ANALYSIS OF THE ATTRIBUTE MODEL WITH QUIET AND NOISY HOUSES

Let us assume:
(1) homogeneous houses in the physical and aesthetic sense which differ only because they can be divided into two mutually exclusive homogeneous classes, noisy and quiet;
(2) stable state conditions, i.e. the noise will continue indefinitely and no changes in noise evaluation will occur;
(3) no frictions, i.e. no moving cost or selling cost;
(4) all people or households have exactly the same evaluation of noisy houses—they regard the noise as exactly equivalent to a reduction of 10% in the value (or rent) of the house;
(5) the supply of houses is fixed in the aggregate and we merely consider variations in the fraction of noisy houses.
Under these conditions we can easily find equilibrium. In Figure 4.1 the aggregate demand for housing at the quiet price is shown by DD and we show the *quiet price* as p_q on the vertical axis. With the use of assumption (4) we can show the noisy price p_n as $0.9p_q$. It follows that for any given p_q there is an infinitely elastic demand for noisy houses at $0.9p_q = p_n$. For any given total number of quiet houses Q_q and noisy houses Q_n we can find the price p_q and so $p_n(= 0.9p_q)$. We are, however, assuming that the demand for housing DD remains fixed whatever the fraction of quiet to noisy houses. The aggregate spending on housing is $p_nQ_n + p_qQ_q$ or $p_q(Q_q + 0.9Q_n)$ and it is clear for a given $(Q_n + Q_q)$ the value of housing will decrease as the fraction of noisy houses increase. Although by the assumption (4)

above people are as well off with a noisy house at a 10 per cent discount as with a quiet house, it follows that the larger the fraction of noisy houses the more money people have available to spend on other goods and services.[1] Of course reciprocally the house-owners' wealth (or rent income) is reduced. It would be most convenient, but perhaps unrealistic, to assume at this

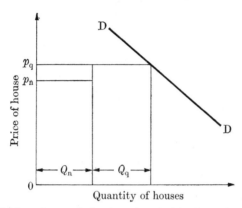

FIG. 4.1. Market demand for housing (with Q_n noisy homes and Q_q quiet homes).

stage that the money value of making the noise to the airlines and passengers is just equal to (or only very slightly more than) the discount on noisy houses, in which case there would be no net aggregate income effects.[2] Thus whatever the fraction of noisy houses, the demand curve stays put. If one were to assume that the aggregate value of making the noise was considerably greater than the differential in house prices, one would have to show an outward shift in the demand for housing since total income has increased. We shall ignore these income effects in this study on the presumption that they are not an important feature determining the relative price and quantities.

In the simple model the cost of an increase in the fraction of noisy houses is calculated as $(0\cdot9p_q)(\Delta Q_n)$, where ΔQ_n is the absolute change in the number of noisy houses. This concept, the change in the total depreciation of residential property due

---

[1] Note that this is not an income effect in the traditional use of that term.
[2] It is also convenient to assume that the distribution effects on the demand for houses are zero.

to noise, is one that was used in the short-list selection procedures of the Roskill Commission.[3] It has the great advantage of simplicity and might be thought appropriate where there is need for a speedy decision on a lengthy list of options—as in the case of the 85 sites surveyed by the Commission. But the disadvantages are such that this simple concept cannot be used where any comparisons of less than an order of magnitude are required. We return to this comparison below.

PERTURBABLES AND IMPERTURBABLES

Perhaps the most discredited assumption of the above list is (5) which supposes that people all have the same evaluation of noise. Clearly any theory or evaluation that carries forward such a manifest absurdity cannot retain our confidence. There is ample evidence that people vary considerably in their reaction to noise. Some are quite imperturbable while others become agitated by any noise however muted. Thus the amount which people would be willing to pay for a quiet life varies. Some, the "imperturbables", will pay nothing; others such as those who cannot bear the stamping of cats will pay a lot. These conditions are illustrated in Figure 4.2(a), which shows the demand curve for noisy houses, and Figure 4.2(b) showing the demand for quiet houses. The demand curve for noisy houses is drawn on the assumption that the price of quiet houses is fixed at p_q^0. If noise is not a "good thing" for anyone the demand curve for noisy houses will not rise above p_q^0.[4] Thus if in Figure 4.2(a) there are Q_n' families in the population who are absolutely imperturbable, a minute price differential is enough to induce them to buy noisy houses. It follows therefore that if the number of noisy houses is less than Q_n' there will be only a minute differential between the prices of noisy and quiet houses. When the stock of noisy houses is less than the number of imperturbables the cost of a (small) variation in noise is virtually zero.

It is more interesting, however, to explore the general case when the quantity of noisy houses exceeds the number of imperturbables—as in the case of Q_n^0 in Figure 4.2(a). Then

---

[3] Roskill Report, pp. 180–8.

[4] Incidentally, this is a question of fact. It is known, for example, that some people actually like noise (and especially making noise). Those who like noise and produce it would have to bear the cost of privately producing noise and insulating their neighbours from it.

noisy houses will sell at p_n^0. One must observe, however, that
the demand for quiet houses depends upon the price of noisy
houses—hence it is written as $D_q(p_n^0)$. Clearly, if we hold to our
assumption that there is a substantial number of imperturbables the demand for quiet houses will become very elastic as
p_q^0 approaches the fixed value p_n^0. As the price of a quiet house

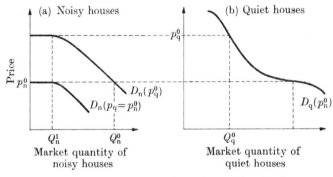

FIG. 4.2. Market demands for noisy and quiet houses.

drops fractionally below the fixed price of a noisy house the
whole imperturbable demand for houses will be concentrated in
the quiet sector. For prices of quiet houses below p_n^0, therefore,
the demand for quiet houses (D_q) is simply the aggregate market
demand for the stock of quiet houses. Noisy houses will be left
empty. This demand curve for noisy houses will fall as the price
of quiet houses is reduced, until when $p_q = p_n^0$ the demand for
noisy houses is zero at p_n^0. The demand curve for noisy houses
with the price of quiet houses fixed at $p_q = p_n^0$ is shown by the
broken line $D_n(p_q = p_n^0)$.

We can now trace the effects of an increase in the fraction of
noisy houses on the relative price differential. In order to
simplify the geometrical representation we assume, perhaps
realistically, that these are no absolute imperturbables but that
reaction to noise is a continuum. Thus the demand for noisy
houses is represented as a line always sloping downwards in
Figure 4.3. If therefore a given number of houses which had
been quiet now become noisy we would expect the price of
noisy houses to fall and that of quiet houses to rise. But the

relative differential would be less than that shown by the original demand curves since those are drawn on the assumption of fixed prices for the other kind of house. Thus the demand curve for quiet houses would fall in response to a lower price for noisy houses, and the demand for noisy houses would rise since quiet houses have become more expensive.

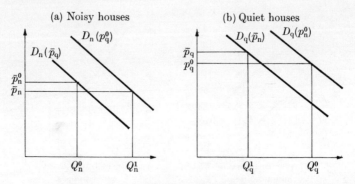

FIG. 4.3. Adjustments of market demands for noisy and quiet Houses.

The equilibrium would therefore be given by $(\bar{p}_q, \bar{p}_n)$ at the fixed quantities (Q'_q, Q'_n).

A few qualitative conclusions can be drawn at this stage. First, if the increase in the quantity of noisy houses relative to the total quantity of houses is small then the price differential will not change significantly. For small relative changes the differential can be taken as a constant. Thus the size of the relevant housing market is an important consideration. Secondly, if the elasticity of substitution at the existing relative quantity of noisy houses is high, then again the variation in the demand for noise will not much change the differential. The demand curves will shift sufficiently to leave the existing differential unchanged.

THE DERIVED DEMAND FOR THE ATTRIBUTE A QUIET LIFE

It is possible to derive a demand for the attribute a quiet life from this formulation. Consider again the demand for noisy houses given a fixed price of quiet houses. Now it is clear that

there are people who would not live in a noisy house even if it
were free. So sensitive are these people that they would be
prepared to pay the whole price of a quiet house for the benefit
of a quiet life. Thus their marginal evaluation of quiet is given
by the value p_q^0. It is not merely conceivable but, if we believe
what they say, even likely that some people would have to be

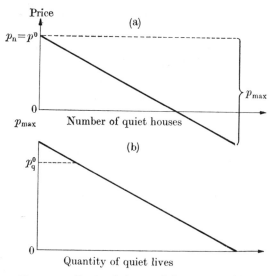

FIG. 4.4. Derived demand for a quiet life.

paid to induce them to occupy a noisy house. Let us suppose
that in the whole population there is a sensitive millionaire who
would be willing to pay most (p_{max} in Figure 4.4) for a quiet
life. Then we can draw up the demand for a quiet life with our
sensitive millionaire at the zero (p_{max}) point and the imperturbables at the other extreme willing to pay nothing.[5]

SUPPLY CONDITIONS IN THE ATTRIBUTE MODEL

In concluding this discussion of the attribute model of the
effects of a certain number of houses once quiet becoming

[5] Again the reader will recall acquaintances who actually enjoy noise and
presumably would pay a negative price for quiet! It is also necessary to note
that those who say that they greatly value a quiet life usually have it in mind
that someone else should pay for their peace; it is easy to demonstrate that
many such peaceniks could buy virtually complete peace but do not do so,
thus we may take their protestations with a large pinch of salt.

noisy, let me stress again that it matters greatly whether that number is a substantial fraction of the total market or whether it can be taken to be a small proportional change. If it is a small proportional change (or there are high elasticities of substitution) we do not have to face the difficulties of measuring the demand curve for quiet in order to evaluate the effects of the change. We can take the price differential as given.

Whether this is a sensible approximation depends, of course, on the facts of the case. As an illustration consider the case of London's third airport. At a maximum this would have affected some 60,000 households and the average number for the four short-listed sites is about 25,000. The total number of houses that comprise essentially the housing market of the area must be considered as at least twenty times that number. The substitution elasticities between one area and another in London's commuter belt according to both estate agents and other available knowledge are large. To dispute that the relative effects are "small" is to impale oneself on "Morton's Fork". If the area is small for which one must consider demand conditions, so that the proportional change is large, then it must follow that the demand is very elastic since there are so many good alternatives outside the area. If, on the other hand, one agrees that it is large then one must accept that the proportional change is small.[6] Thus we may conclude that the typical case is one of approximately a fixed noise depreciation differential.

The role and importance of the free reactions of the supply of houses should be taken into account. Clearly adaptations in the supply of dwellings will take place. One obvious possibility in the short run is the insulation of houses against noise. This will differentiate the housing stock and enable some adjustment to be made without incurring the costs of moving house.

In the long term (and in the absence of land-zoning) one would expect an adjustment of land use from noise-sensitive to noise-insensitive activities—from housing to industrial uses. The substantial investment of a fixed long-term character in housing makes this switch very costly in any period other than

---

[6] I put this dilemma to Mr. S. P. C. Plowden, the witness for the British Airport Authority, during the course of the hearings at Stage V of the Roskill Commission. See Roskill Commission (1970b), pp. 23–30.

a very long one. Transfers from agricultural uses to industrial development are easier but of little interest in this context.

Land-zoning complicates the problem by creating artificially "floating values" for land that has the much-sought development certificate or zoning classification. Typically planning authorities try to prevent building of houses in the noise shadow of airports and even entertain ideas about buying up existing property that is much affected by noise. Typically also planning fails to achieve its aims, but provides much friction in the system. We return to this problem in chapter 7.

It has also been argued that people gradually adjust and get used to aircraft noise. They learn to live with it. Habits change and affect preferences. In principle the approach adopted in this model assumes that such an acclimatization to noise is known to the individual or family in advance. They know that they will "get used to it". Thus this effect is already incorporated in the present values of noise nuisance and does not formally require further development.

A GENERAL EQUILIBRIUM MODEL WITH VARIABLE NOISE LEVELS[7]

One of the difficulties with the analysis so far is that by using the traditional demand and supply analytical framework rather stringent assumptions have had to be made in order to get the problem into a two- or three-dimensional world. This often does no harm, but occasionally the essence of the problem may be lost by such a simplification. One of the purposes of this discussion is to show where such simplifications may be misleading.

We can still examine only a very special model; otherwise we simply get complicated but very general results. But the aspects of the problem now investigated are *different* from those explored above with the ordinary demand and supply curve technique. One of the assumptions which we have made above is that houses are divided into two homogeneous classes as far as noise is concerned—they are either noisy or quiet. But with

[7] I am grateful to A. Mitchell Polinsky and Steven Shavell, both visiting scholars at the Urban Institute in the Summer of 1972, for convincing me that it would be better to state the model formally; I am now sure that they are right.

this assumption one cannot adduce the amount (or strictly the median amount) which people would be willing to pay to avoid the noise from the rate of depreciation of house prices in the afflicted zone.[8] The question arises whether this criticism is valid if, for a given income, the householder has the choice of a more or less continuous adjustment of the amount of quiet he may buy—for example he may purchase a house 5 miles from the runway or directly underneath the flight path or anywhere in between. We shall now show that, for the special Cobb–Douglas utility function, the depreciation on house prices is independent of the "price" of quiet and that it does measure the mean value of the distribution of people according to their sensitivity to noise. Of course such a nice neat result is a consequence of the Cobb–Douglas assumption, but it is at least qualitatively clear that similar plausible utility functions will give rise to broadly the same conclusions.[9]

It is convenient first to set out the model on the assumption that all households have the same income. This gets rid of the nuisance variable (at least it is a nuisance in this context) income and so we can think of the analysis being applied to one price-class of houses.[10] It is also convenient to restrict the goods considered to two—a composite good (bread) that includes all things other than quiet which the household buys, and the other good quiet. In other words we do not analyse the joint-supply effects which arise because one buys a house and residential quiet at the same time and perhaps only in certain specific proportions; it is supposed that there is an open choice of any amount of house with any amount of quiet and so quiet is treated as any other homogeneous good which can be bought

[8] To avoid misrepresentation let me quote the Roskill Report, § 15, p. 270: "We are aware that the Research Team did not substantiate…its assumption that the median of the noise annoyance distribution is associated with the average house price depreciation."

[9] One particular "irrational" behaviour pattern will give the same results as the Cobb–Douglas. Suppose that each family with the same income chooses the degree of quiet at random; in particular imagine that there is an equal chance for all the quantities of quiet available. Then we may show that the *market* relationships have approximately the same form as those developed below. See Gary S. Becker (1962), pp.1–13.

[10] Note that there is a practical difficulty since the price class of houses will reflect the noise depreciation—and so on the average poorer people will live in the noisier houses. This is a version of the ubiquitous regression fallacy which we do not pursue here.

by the individual in any quantities at the going price on the market. The primary purpose of the model is to examine the patterns of behaviour of people according to their taste for quiet or according to their different degrees of noise sensitivity. Individuals vary according to their taste for a quiet life.

Let $U^i = x_i^{1-b_i} q_i^{b_i}$ be the utility function of the ith individual, where x is the number of loaves of bread (a composite consumption good), q is the number of homogeneous units of quiet, and b_i is the constant—the "taste" for quiet—for the ith individual of whom there are N in the economy ($i = 1, 2, \ldots n$). Let us suppose that the price of bread is unity per loaf and that the price of quiet is p. For all individuals we suppose that they have the same income:

$$y = x_i + pq_i \qquad i = (1, 2, \ldots, N).$$

Then we can solve easily to get the demand functions

$$q_i = b_i y/p \quad \text{and} \quad x_i = y(1-b_i).$$

If the total supply of quiet and bread is fixed and denoted by Q and X respectively, the equilibrium conditions are

$$\sum_i q_i = Q \quad \text{and} \quad \sum_i x_i = X.$$

Thus we find that

$$p = \frac{X(\sum b_i)}{Q \sum (1-b_i)} = kX/Q \quad \text{and} \quad k = (\sum b_i)/\sum(1-b_i),$$

where k represents the (constant) taste for quiet in the population. The relative supply of quiet affects the price in a very simple way.

With the production transformation function $f(X, Q) = 0$, we find the slope of the frontier dX/dQ. Then if in a perfect market the amount of quiet and bread are 'correctly' produced, this slope will be equal to the price of quiet:

$$p = kX/Q = dX/dQ.$$

So in this special case we can write the taste parameter

$$k = d \ln X/d \ln Q.$$

Now consider the noise taste coefficient b_i. We note that:

$$b_i = pq_i/y \qquad (i = 1, 2, \ldots N).$$

Thus the fraction of income spent on quiet is equal to the noise taste parameter. (Alternatively we can regard the noise taste parameter as a measure of the perturbability of the person i due to noise.) Now examine the mean value of the b_is over the population, i.e.

$$\frac{1}{N}\sum_i b_i = \frac{p}{Ny}\sum_i q_i;$$

and so:

$$\bar{b} = p\bar{q}/y$$

where $\bar{b}$ is the mean of the b_is, and $\bar{q}$ is the mean of the q_is, and the fraction spent on quiet for the population as a whole gives the average value of the noise sensitivity coefficient.

This model appears to provide a theoretical rationalization for the assumption that the *average noise depreciation on houses is a good measure of the mean value of the distribution of the noise coefficient* in the Cobb–Douglas utility functions. But since we have held income constant throughout the analysis, such a mean value should be restricted to a particular income group (or somehow the effects of income on the purchase of quiet should be eliminated).[11]

We can now examine some the characteristics of the model. First let us consider the case which we pursued with the attribute model where only a relatively small number of households in this community are subject to higher noise—and let us suppose that the number so affected is sufficiently small for their behaviour to have *no* discernable effect on the price of quiet. Then those suffering the new noise will now be spending too little on quiet; so they will move to a quieter neighbourhood so that the amount spent on quiet is the same as it was before. The noisy houses they vacate will then be occupied by people who spend infinitesimally less on quiet than before, and so the adjustment is completed with approximately the same price of quiet as before. This, as we should expect, is the result we obtained from the attribute model.

Now, secondly, consider the case where the new noise affects a relatively large number of households. If the price of quiet remained the same they would now try to buy back some of

[11] We can hold the income of those who suffer the noise constant by supposing that they are compensated with a lump sum for the noise so that their income is the same as it was before the new noise.

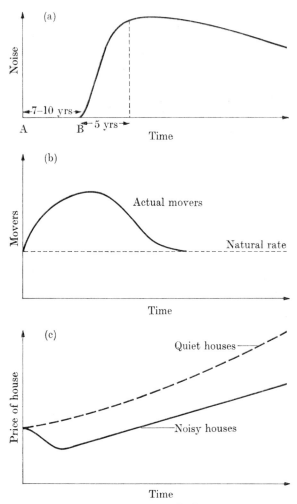

FIG. 4.5. Dynamics of adjustment.

their lost peace by attempting to restore their usual expenditure on quiet; thus they would make bids for quiet houses. But this additional demand will *increase the price of quiet* (and of quiet houses). Those who at present live in houses not physically affected by the new noise will find that at the new higher price of quiet they are spending too much on quiet. They will therefore move to somewhat noisier houses so that their

5

expenditure on quiet is the same as it was before. Thus if the aggregate quantity of quiet has decreased 10 per cent then the price of quiet will rise 10 per cent and everyone will change houses so that the amount of quiet he buys has decreased by 10 per cent to give the same expenditure on quiet. This is a result which is different from that of the attribute model; with attributes supply affects expenditure, but with the Cobb–Douglas continuum model such supply changes do not cause any change in spending.

This frictionless model has no movement costs and assumes perfect knowledge. It seems quite ludicrous to imagine that every time there is a change in the amount of noise everyone changes house! The excuse is that these flighty people are simple to model. And the theory does capture some of the essential features of the house-noise allocation process. Although we cannot imagine everyone moving because of noise we know that much movement takes place for other reasons. In those cases the movement costs and some of the search costs are already incurred, and so for each change of residence the household will be free to buy as much quiet as it wishes. In the United States, for example, it is likely that after a period of 10 years some 60–70 per cent of households have moved at least once—so that after this time there will be a substantial adjustment in response to the noise source along the lines suggested by the theory. It is important then to bear in mind that the theory may be useful in the long run but not for short-run predictions.

THE COSTS OF ADJUSTMENT TO A NEW NOISE SOURCE

So far the analysis has been conducted in terms of the conventional framework of static supply and demand theory. Now one must take into account the dynamics of the fact that a new noise source is to be imposed on an area hitherto quiet. It is simplest to begin with the assumption that no one knows that the airport is going to be located in the new area until a certain date; then everyone knows that fact. Furthermore, all households have exactly the same correct expectations of the physical (acoustical) and economic consequences of noise.

First we may describe the physical measure of noise—as it

emerges from the Noise Number Index or the Noise Exposure Forecast of any other similar rating. This is shown in the form of a time series in section (a) of Figure 4.5. The delay from the announcement date at A to the opening of the airport at B is the construction period—perhaps some 7–10 years for most normal airports. Assuming that the airport is no white elephant the major noise impact would be felt quite quickly after opening.[12] The build-up of aircraft movements would be rapid. But also one would anticipate that the effects of quieter engines would begin to be felt gradually, as the old turbo-jets are phased out and engines with a high by-pass ratio become increasingly common. Thus the NNI index may begin early to decline, and so the future noise profile is humped. With perfect knowledge of the future, this profile would be assimilated in the present value calculations.

In Figure 4.5(b) we show the rates of people moving out of and into the affected area. These movements are expressed as a certain percentage each year. First we must take into account the *natural movers*. These are moves that would occur even in the absence of any airport and include movements because of new employments, new housing needs, and so on. This is an important element of the process since those who would have moved even if there had been no airport have an opportunity to find (and pay for) a quiet house if they so wish. The movement costs are incurred in any case and cannot be attributed to the advent of the airport. But even these natural movers do suffer from the effect of noise blight on their property. In addition to the natural movers there are the noise-induced movers—we can call them *noise movers* for short. People will move if the present values of their expected noise-annoyance evaluations exceed the present values of a combination of differential surplus, noise depreciation, and removal costs. The gain from a move at a particular time is calculated as:

present value of future noise   *less*   present value of costs of
    annoyance at t moving at time t (i.e.
                                             surplus loss, deprecia-
                                             tion, and moving costs).

---

[12] It may be claimed, however, that such an assumption is unrealistic and does not correspond with observed behaviour.

In practice, one would expect some people to move before the airport opens. There will be a distribution of expectations of the values that enter the above inequality, since the moving and searching process is one that inevitably involves time. A householder may just see the opportunity he was looking for early in the search process or he may find no suitable residence until the airport is open and in operation. Thus the pattern of movers would be expected to be something like that shown in Figure 4.5(b). In the calculations of the model, with its more stringent assumptions, however, it is more convenient to assume that no noise moves take place before the date of opening of the airport, because for a fixed future pattern of D, S, and R no potential noise mover would gain by "jumping the gun".

Finally, in Figure 4.5(c) we sketch the price depreciation due to noise as it will develop over time. The vertical axis measures the real price of houses over time; it is commonly thought that the price of houses will increase faster than the index of prices as a whole and this has been shown by the rising trend. Again there are difficulties in plotting the early stages of the process of adjustment to the announcement of a new airport. In the absence of uncertainty, however, there is no reason why there should be a yawning gap between the price of quiet and price of noisy houses. One would expect that the gap, however, would rapidly widen as the opening day approached. There is also good reason for supposing that the gap will widen over time not only absolutely but also relatively. This widening will be due to the fact that (1) incomes are growing over time and residential quiet is a luxury good, and (2) the relative scarcity of quiet environments is increasing (although on this point of course much depends on the success of noise-control methods). On the other hand (3) we would expect that quieter aircraft would reduce the noise differential. Acceptance of these arguments of course implies that we also value quiet (N) at a rate that increases over time to reflect higher real incomes. Many people argue that the present (1972) obsessive concern with the environment is not a mere passing fad and that tastes will change over time so that people will value quiet more highly than they do now at a given level of income. This would produce an ever-widening gap. As far as one can judge then it seems that the balance is in favour of a widening gap. But evidence is required to sharpen this conjecture.

Now we can proceed to an evaluation of the new noise source. There are three categories of household in the analysis:

(a) The *natural movers* who would have moved in any case. Their costs are simply the depreciation that the property which they sell has suffered as a consequence of the decision to locate an airport.

(b) The *stayers* who will suffer a noise annoyance measured by the present value of the discounted future stream of annoyance.

(c) The *noise movers* who move because of the noise, and will lose their differential surplus, the noise depreciation of their house, and the removal costs.

The calculation of the costs appropriate to each category is a complicated exercise but it involves no new points of principle and we relegate the details to the note at the end of chapter 5.

One feature of this dynamic process should be borne in mind. The process of natural movement enables the noise-sensitive people ultimately to move out of the area even if they do not fall under the classification of noise-movers—that is to say even if their noise evaluation is not high enough to overcome the inertia of capital and surplus loss and removal costs. The sorting process will still go on—but much more slowly—under the natural migration patterns. It follows, therefore, that the longer the time lead between announcement of the airport decision and the flights and the greater the rate of normal movements, the smaller the impact of noise will be. In the long run, assuming that the whole population have some propensity to move naturally, the sorting will be complete. Only the imperturbables will be found in the noisy areas.

CONCLUDING REMARKS

The results of this chapter divide into two broad groups. First there are the conclusions of the partial and general equilibrium analysis. These show the application of traditional tools of economic price theory to the case of noise nuisance. Secondly, there is an attempt to put these results into a process of adjustment to a newly imposed noise source.

It is worth recording that throughout we were concerned with positive analysis. The theory attempts to predict what will happen in fact in response to a new noise nuisance. There is no pretence to provide a normative analysis to predict what is desirable. Even in the discussion of the measure of the costs of noise the concern is with an objective measure of how much people would be prepared to pay (or receive in compensation). There is no presumption that either the creation of a noise source, or the charging of noise-makers, or the compensation of those who suffer are "good things". The measures of price of quiet and cost of noise are meant to be objective predictions not normative prescriptions for policy. Whether the predictions of the theory are correct depends on the facts (see chapter 6). But if the facts are consistent with the predictions these may then serve as the basis for normative policy proposals. Different people, however, will arrive at different prescriptions from the same facts.

But even if one rejects the price and cost evidence as a substantive basis for policy (and there are many who state that a quiet life is "without price"), it is difficult to believe that anyone would accept that the price and cost effects are of no interest whatsoever. One may well believe that in some ideal state people should value quiet at a far higher value than they appear to place upon it in the markets of our time. But even so a knowledge of what people *do* is a standard of reference for the most Utopian idealist. Reality should always be relevant.

CHAPTER 5

Measurement and Identification
of Noise Costs

THE PROBLEM

THE theory of chapters 3 and 4 has provided a way of approaching the data of the real world. We now know what effects to look for, and how the material should be organized. The theory predicts that there will be some relative depreciation in the price of houses which come under a new noise shadow—provided that there are a sufficiently large number of people sensitive to noise in relation to the number of quiet houses available. Correspondingly, houses in an old high-noise area will sell at a discount compared with similar quiet property.

These price differentials are market phenomena and should be revealed by market data. It is true, however, that in practice there are many other effects which affect house prices and which have to be somehow held constant. The relative price of quiet may be obscured by all the other factors that determine the price of a dwelling. But the problem is then one of statistical distillation.

Movement costs (R) are in a similar category to the house price noise depreciation. They can be observed on the market but there are many "other factors" that need to be eliminated to get an appropriate measure. One of the particular difficulties about movement cost is that the expense of searching for a buyer and seller involves not merely money and time, but also frustration. The value of such activities as negotiating, etc., is difficult to observe directly.

The differential surplus (S) is of course even more difficult to observe. In principle one would like to carry out experiments by holding all other prices constant and gradually raising the price of houses in a particular neighbourhood. Then one would be able to measure the differential surplus for each person. (Note, however, that such a measure would be the higher differential surplus rather than the lower one as defined on pp. 33–4 above.) In practice, one has difficulties in finding data for situations of the kind, and as we shall see one is reduced to using more dubious methods. But measurability for S is possible in principle, and we shall shortly discuss the methods to be used.

On the other hand, it seems that there is no way of directly observing N, the evaluation which an individual puts on aircraft noise. We know that it varies from one individual to another and that it would be proper to describe it as a distribution. Although attempts have been made to measure the distribution by direct inquiry and in particular its mean by some form of questionnaire, it would be wrong to suppose that they have any substantive theoretical or empirical basis. Some other approach is required.

MEASURING THE NOISE VALUATION (N)

We first begin with the attribute model discussed on pp. 42–9 above. Thus we imagine that people have a choice between one sort of noisy house and one sort of quiet house; there is no in-between. Let us suppose that the distribution described in Figure 5.1 is appropriate to describe the distribution of people according to their valuation N for a certain specified noisiness (NNI). Suppose also that they have a given differential surplus (S) and moving costs (R) which are assumed the same for all persons, and the same difference in price between noisy and quiet houses. Then we know the values of S, R, and D. If we now observe that (say) 10 per cent of the people move because of the noise, then this will give one measure to help locate the distribution of people with respect to their valuation of noise (N) in Figure 5.1.[1]

In principle, if one had another airport in another location such that there were quite large differences in D (the difference in prices of quiet and noisy houses) one would be able to generate another observation of the distribution. Thus with a sufficient number of observations one could derive the distribution. Of course it would be immensely valuable if one knew the form of the distribution; for example, if one knew that it was a

---

[1] The ideas in these paragraphs were first put by me at the Stage V hearings: Roskill Commission (1970b), day 54, pp. 86–91.

rectangular distribution with the lowest value of $N = 0$, then one observation would be sufficient to locate the distribution.[2]

The method of generating the distribution of N seems in principle unexceptionable, but it does hinge on a number of perhaps questionable presumptions. First, it must be held that the distribution of people according to their N measure does

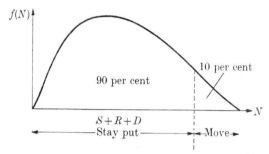

FIG. 5.1. Frequency distribution $f(N)$ of households with respect to their valuation of noise (N) for a given NNI.

not change from one area to another. This implies that if one area is rural and the other urban there is no adjustment such as those with a high N moving into the country and the low N people buying houses in town. Secondly, the proportion who move may be motivated by effects other than aircraft noise; for example, the movement may occur because of the general change in the area and this may differ between different sites. Thirdly, and most important, this method of finding the distribution of N makes impossible demands on the data. It requires one to measure the "movers-due-to-noise" over a period of (say) ten years for different airport sites; a major study indeed!

Although one may doubt whether it is worth-while to attempt to establish the distribution of N from such movement data, it *is* desirable to check any distribution of N, derived from other sources, to see whether it is broadly consistent with the available movement data. The movement predictions may be used to test any alternative hypothesis.

[2] Oddly enough, this rectangular distribution of N will give rise to the linear demand curve for quiet which was sketched above, but such mathematical convenience does not necessarily fit the facts.

It is not surprising, however, that in practice the "movers method" has not been systematically explored. The research worker is tempted to capitalize on what data are available in order to construct a distribution of households by N. The most widely available data are statistics derived from psycho-sociological studies of the reaction of people to noise.[3]

These show that different people have widely varying degrees of noise tolerance quantified in terms of their reaction to a given NNI rating.[4] Some correspondence between the reaction scale and the valuation of noise scale (N) would then permit the translation of the distribution of people by their reaction to noise into the distribution by the amount they would be willing to accept in compensation for the noise.

This was the approach adopted by the Roskill Research Team but ultimately rejected by the Commission.[5] The Research Team assumed that the N distribution was such that its median money value was equal to the difference between the prices of noisy and quiet houses. Various rationalizations of this assumption were given. For example, it was argued that in order for noise-affected property to find as ready a sale as quiet houses, buyers who were sensitive to noise would need to balance against those who were relatively insensitive. Thus to preserve the same saleability the noise depreciation on the house would divide the prospective buyers into roughly two equal groups— hence the median assumption. This argument, however, has little substance since, if the distribution of N has a high variance, then there will be very energetic bidding from the imperturb-ables and the price differential would close. In other words, the differential depreciation would be determined by the number of imperturbables in the market. This brings us back to the relative supply effects discussed in chapter 4.

Nevertheless, it is worth-while examining the consequences of the median assumption in terms of our simple attribute model.

In Figure 5.2(a) we have reproduced the demand for noisy houses for a fixed price of quiet houses. To simplify matters we ignore movement costs and the differential surplus so we suppose

[3] See Wilson Committee (1963).
[4] See chapter 2.
[5] See *Roskill Report*, § 12.54–8.

that both are zero. Further to simplify the exposition suppose
that the distribution is symmetric so that the median is equal
to the mean. We suppose that there are fixed numbers of $0Q$
households in the community and that even the most sensitive
will pay a positive price for a noisy house at Q. Then if the
demand is linear over its whole length from A to C' (Figure
5.2(a)) the Research Team's assumption that the depreciation

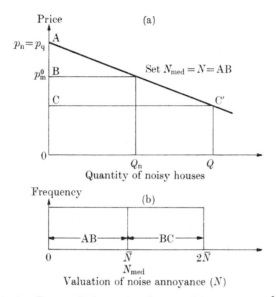

FIG. 5.2. (a) Demand for noisy homes (given $p_n = p_q^0$), (b) N
distribution $f(N)$ for a linear demand curve given $N_{med} = AB$.

measured the medium noise disbenefit would be consistent with
the N distribution which is given in Figure 5.2(b). The Research
Team identified the value AB in Figure 5.2(a) as the median
of the distribution of N ($N = N_{med}$).

This analysis shows there is no clear reason why the N
distribution should have the median value.[6] Consider for
example two communities each of which has exactly the same
distribution of N but the first has suffered considerably from

[6] This was argued during the Stage V Hearings of the Roskill Commission
and especially forcibly by the witness Mr. S. P. C. Plowden. His contribution
to this whole analysis of aircraft noise was particularly valuable to the
Commission.

noise and experienced a considerable price depreciation of noisy houses, whereas the other has suffered little or no noise and its few noisy houses are occupied at a very small discount by the imperturbables. Clearly, it is wrong to attribute a different noise sensitivity to these communities because of the different amounts of noise imposed on them.[7] The inclusion of movement costs R and the differential surplus S merely adds complications; the essential nature of the argument remains unchanged. We conclude, therefore, that the only basis on which the attribute model can be fitted to the data is by measuring the number of noise movers. If, however, one adopts a medium-noise-disbenefit assumption like that of the Roskill Research Team, then it is necessary to see whether the number who actually do move corresponds with the number predicted by the model.[8] Only then can one have confidence in its predictions.

An alternative approach to the measurement of N was carried out by Mr. S. P. C. Plowden.[9] It was based on a survey of households. The respondents were asked to imagine a situation where they were on the point of moving to a new house that met all the main requirements. They were then asked what price discount they would require on their new house if they then found it was subject to three different degrees of aircraft noise. The advantages and disadvantages of the survey method for discovering hypothetical values are well known and will not be retold here. The response to the survey suggests that no great confidence can be invested in the results. Approximately one-half of the respondents were unwilling to quote a money figure in their answers. The reasons for this were probably due to the form of the question. But of course there are genuine doubts about questions that depend on people being able to project themselves into a hypothetical environment which is perhaps far from their experiences. The reported results of the survey were of the same order of magnitude as those used by the

[7] Indeed one would conjecture then if there is some migration between the communities, the peaceful community would have a higher mean N distribution. We return to this point below in discussing the imposition of noise on a hitherto very peaceful area.

[8] This was essentially the suggestion that I put before the public hearings—Roskill Commission (1970b), day 54.

[9] Roskill Commission (1970b), Documents 5006A-C.

Research Team and one may readily conjecture why this is so.

Again it is possible to test the assessments of N from the survey: we could find the predicted number of movers and examine to see whether this actual number is consistent with the number predicted by the model.

To sum up, the attribute model does give rise to a singularly difficult measurement problem in calibrating the noise annoyance measure. No good reasons can be discovered for any *a priori* calibration, such as the median depreciation assumption, and the only acceptable approach is the seemingly very difficult one of fitting the N distribution with respect to observed movement rates. However, in the attribute model we ignore the information contained in the choice between more or less noisy houses. To this we now turn.

MEASURING NOISE NUISANCE WHEN THERE IS A CHOICE BETWEEN VARIABLE NOISE LEVELS

So far the attribute model has been couched in terms of a *particular* level of noise; we have supposed that the N referred to a particular NNI or CNR condition, and examined the choice, whether to leave or stay, with this particular NNI in mind. We know, however, that the householder has a wide variety of choices of degrees of noisiness—he can choose a house within the 40 to 45 contours which is moderately noisy or he can put up with the bedlam of the 55 NNI contour. This choice is an observable market phenomenon. The question arises whether or not it is possible to use this choice in order to adduce evidence on the values which people place on the noise nuisance N.

The Cobb–Douglas general equilibrium model on pp. 51–2 above gave us a method of examining these choices. It was shown that the expenditure on quiet of an individual householder reflected his "taste" for quiet (b_i). But the individual expenditure was composed of two elements, the given market price for quiet and the number of units of quiet that he chose to buy.

With this interpretation of the model we can now examine the criticisms discussed above. It is now easy to see how confusion was spread by the critics of the proposition that the noise depreciation measured the median noise disbenefit. If we restrict the argument to merely two classes, noisy and quiet houses, then the depreciation on the noisy house measures not only the expenditure on quiet but also the price of quiet. Now the price of quiet is clearly determined by the relative supplies of quiet and other goods—in particular noisy and quiet houses. Thus in this all-or-nothing attribute case the expenditure on quiet must be determined by the relative supplies. As we demonstrated above, *if* everyone is required to buy either a noisy or a quiet house and there are no half-noisy, quarter-noisy, etc., options, then there is no justification for supposing that the depreciation figures tell one anything about the noise-disbenefit distribution.

But such a model is a travesty of the facts. One can buy more or less as much quiet as one wishes; this must be considered as one essential feature of the market for quiet. In our version q is a variable not a zero/unity attribute. With our special Cobb–Douglas model, whatever the price of quiet the consumer will adjust his spending so that his expenditure on quiet remains the same. The amount spent (for a given income) is independent of the price since the elasticity of demand for the individual is -1.[10]

The Cobb-Douglas and the all-or-nothing model represent particular cases; the Cobb–Douglas might well be a good approximation to the facts, whereas the all-or-nothing model certainly is not. The Cobb–Douglas has a demand for quiet of -1 for each individual in the relevant population. And although for a given income level different households will spend different fractions of their income on quiet in accordance with their taste (b_i) for quiet relative to bread, the amount spent by a particular family will be the same; thus aggregate spending of quiet will be the same for the given income group whatever the price of quiet.

There is no overriding theoretical reason for supposing that the elasticity of demand for quiet is unity or that the utility function has a Cobb–Douglas form. The evidence for example may show that there is a substantial increase in the amount spent on quiet as the price increases—indicating an inelastic

[10] In the all-or-nothing case the elasticity of demand for the individual is normally zero, except when the infinitesimal price change just induces him to buy a quiet house, and then it is infinite.

demand. However, if we interpret the variable q as a measure of freedom from aircraft noise, then it seems implausible to suppose that the demand for such a specific form of quiet will have a very low elasticity since there are many other varieties of 'quiet' and other environmental features which one can substitute (such as freedom from smell or visual intrusion) and there is always the possibility of relief by insulation.[11] The evidence shows that the price elasticity of demand for housing is approximately -1 and since "quiet" is one of the bundle of goods bought with a house it seems at least plausible to suppose that the price elasticity of quiet is in the same region. In the absence of evidence to the contrary one may take a unity elasticity as a reasonable first approximation. If it is convincingly discredited by the evidence then the case must be reopened.

Assuming, therefore, that the distribution of b_i is independent of the price of quiet, we can illustrate the form of the distribution in Figure 5.3. At the lower end are the people who spend virtually nothing on quiet so that their b_is are approximately zero. These imperturbables will live in the very noisy houses which suffer maximum noise depreciation. Most people, however, live in areas that are not much affected by aircraft noise and consequently spend sizeable fractions of their income on quiet in the sense that they choose to occupy the more expensive houses away from the flight paths. Thus we should expect the mode of the distribution to lie near to the maximum value of b_i, say b_{max}. (It will later be shown that b_{max} in the United Kingdom and possibly also in the United States corresponds to about 7 per cent of income in the upper income brackets and probably about 2 or 3 per cent of the lower-income groups.) If, as we shall later show, the commodity 'residential quiet' is a luxury good then the distribution of b_i for lower incomes will lie to the left of the distribution for high incomes— the fraction spent on quiet will be smaller as income diminishes.

The scale on which we have measured b_i in the above Figure 5.3 might also be used to measure the number of units of

[11] This suggests that one might usefully analyse the general "commodity" called 'environmental quiet' which could be defined as a function of freedom from different types of noise—from traffic, from people, from aircraft, etc. This could then be handled by using a separable form of the utility function.

quiet bought (since the price of a unit of quiet is fixed over the cross-section). Alternatively, one may conventionally measure the noisiness by writing the scale in NNI, CNR, or NEF terms in inverse order, that is from right to left. In this model, one would expect to find that for a given noise level and income there would be a number of people indicated by the frequency range who would have a taste for quiet b_i which exactly

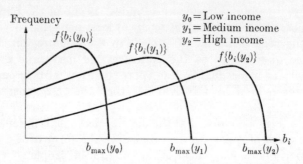

FIG. 5.3. Frequency distribution of b_i, i.e. $f(b_i)$ for given incomes.

corresponds to the fraction of their income that they spend on quiet. A given noise measure and income are sufficient to determine exactly how much people spend on quiet in that category and so determine exactly the noise or quiet taste coefficient. There is no distribution of b_is corresponding to a given income and noisiness in the theoretical model.

The Roskill Research Team, however, did in fact choose to generate a distribution of b_is about a median value for the noise annoyance level. Such a distribution may be rationalized largely by appealing to the facts. Psychological and sociological surveys do appear to show that there is a distribution of people with different noise (or quiet) taste coefficients within a given noise level and income group[12] And of course one can easily see why such a distribution may well be generated by events in the real world. The costs of adjustment—giving up the differential house surplus and incurring movement costs—may be considerable enough to deter would-be movers; and according

---

[12] See in particular McKennell's data as revealed by the Wilson Committee (1963).

to the evidence quite a lot of people make mistakes and misjudge the amount of noise. It does therefore make sense as a first approximation to regard the observed fraction spent on quiet as the mean or median of a distribution of taste coefficients b_i for given income and noisiness. This distribution will take into account the 'other factors' excluded from the model—such as frictions, mistakes, deviations due to measurement errors, lack of knowledge, etc.

As with any other statistical model one would like to carry the analysis further and identify the causes of the deviation between theory and fact; but such a study requires more elaborate models and data. The presumption or at least the hope is that one has captured the essence of the process in the hypotheses so far developed. For practical applications it seems sensible to use the observed fraction spent on quiet as the mean or median value and to use whatever evidence is available from socio-psychological surveys to generate a distribution of taste coefficients (or what corresponds to the same thing, a distribution of amounts which people would spend in a frictionless world and without other factors affecting the decision). It is necessary, however, to use a distribution where there have been stable conditions for some time so that the distribution of sensitivity to noise for a given b_i represents stable-state conditions—normal mistakes and frictions etc.[13]

We can now state the following propositions:

(1) For small changes in Q and X, the value of p may be taken as approximately fixed (the Roskill assumption).

(2) The noise sensitivity coefficient for the ith individual is b_i and is measured by the fraction of income spent on 'quiet', and the distribution of these is in no way affected by the relative supply of quiet for the Cobb–Douglas case where the elasticity of demand for quiet is -1.

(3) It is misleading to suppose that an efficient analysis of noise can be conducted with an 'all-or-nothing' attribute model. One must take into account that noisiness is a variable and

---

[13] It may well be argued that the Research Team in using McKennell's data were reflecting the wide dispersions of the early years of the jet age; there had been insufficient time to make adjustments to a stable state. Consequently the distributions used by the Research Team had a greater dispersion than they would have under normal conditions.

that people can nicely adjust their consumption of 'quiet' accordingly.

(4) Although where noise is a continuum, as in the model of the unit-elasticity Cobb–Douglas type, the fraction of income spent on quiet for a given income and level of income and noisiness is uniquely determined by the value of taste coefficient b_i, in practice one would expect to find a distribution of taste coefficients for a given fraction of income spent on quiet because of other factors omitted from the model. Empirical evidence from socio-psychological studies of noise confirms this. Consequently, it makes sense to use such a distribution of coefficients in practical applications—and this in part rationalizes the approach of the Roskill Research Team.

(5) For the non-Cobb–Douglas case, variations in the relative supply of quiet will affect the price of quiet, but with 'freedom from aircraft noise' as the commodity one would expect the demand to be relatively elastic so that a rise in the price of quiet would be accompanied by a *fall* in the amount spent on quiet. (Only if there is complete *in*elasticity of market demand would one obtain the result derived from the "all-or-nothing" assumption.)

(6) To avoid misunderstanding, it must be stressed that the amount that a household spends on quiet does not measure the amount they would be just *willing* to spend to achieve that level of quiet. As is normally the case the quiet is worth more than they pay on the market but the marginal unit of quiet is just worth the price that is paid for it. If, however, one were evaluating the effects of a substantial change in the quantity and price of quiet, then it would be necessary to measure the consumer surplus lost in the reduction in the quantity of quiet.[14]

MEASUREMENT OF THE DIFFERENTIAL SURPLUS S

In principle the problem with measuring the value of S, the differential surplus which an owner enjoys with his own property, is that it is not normally observable in any market transaction. People who wish to buy houses can acquire them

---

[14] With the unit-elasticity model the amendment is very simple—the difference in the natural logarithms of the prices is multiplied by the total of the b_is and the income level for each income level.

at the market price only from those people who just wish to sell at that price; there is no way of observing at what price other people would be induced to sell. It is known only that such prices would be higher than the price at present ruling on the market.

It might be thought that situations would occur when such surplus values would be revealed. For example property developers frequently acquire property rights over a substantial area of land in order to build estates, office blocks, or factories. One large tract of land is worth more than a number of small plots. As the developer acquires more land the other un-acquired plots become more and more valuable. Consequently the developer will be induced to offer a higher and higher price in order to induce the original owners to sell at the price which would just make them leave. A list of such prices might be thought to sketch out the distribution of S among this group of house-owners and so among property-owners in general. Unfortunately, this is not so. The developer may well be willing to pay considerably more than the owner would normally happily accept. The perspicacious owner will acquire informa-tion on the so-called 'development value' of the site. The owner will then play hard to get in order to raise the offer to somewhere near the maximum which the developer would be willing to pay. In such a game of poker and call-my-bluff the value at which the transaction actually takes place might be anywhere between the owner's own valuation and what the developer is prepared at most to pay.[15] It seems therefore that such acquisition values may be no good guide to the size of the property-owner's differential surplus. Nevertheless, they would provide an upper limit to S. We have not pursued this approach further since such data are protected as commercial secrets and notoriously difficult to acquire.

An alternative approach is to try to adduce what evidence one can about the differential surplus from studies of the market price elasticity of demand for housing. The demand curve for housing describes how much housing people will buy

[15] Even if there were perfect competition among developers for sites, such conditions would still not ensure that the take-over value was the same as the owner's valuation. The spread of information, the use of bluff and threat, and so on, must at some stage become important in any such take-over—just as they are in the more public business of the take-over of companies.

when the price of housing varies for all persons in the market. The market price elasticity of demand would reveal therefore a distribution of the surplus under the assumption that the prices of *all* houses change. The case with which we are concerned, however, is one where only the prices of houses in the noise-affected area change—all other prices of houses in other areas remain the same as before.[16] Since the residents of the noise-affected area have the opportunity to purchase houses in various other areas the elasticity of demand for housing in the affected area will be considerably larger than the elasticity of demand for housing generally to buy houses at the old price in other areas, one may confidently assert that consequently the values for the differential surplus will be *less* than those implied by the general market elasticities of demand. However, it is an approach worth exploring briefly here.

The evidence suggests that the long-run price elasticity of demand for housing is about −1 or perhaps a little less.[17] Consequently we may use this value to generate the *maximum* values of the distribution of S. A random sample of people or householders might reasonably be expected to have surplus values no larger than those implied by a −1 elasticity of demand. The use of these too-high values in the noise model would generate too few movements since the model would predict that people would stay and suffer whereas in reality they would move.[18]

In the absence of any suitable market observations of the differential surplus, the final resort is to construct a sample survey of house-owners and renters in order to find what price they would take if a developer were willing to make an offer—excluding any taxes, levies, and removal expenses. This approach was used in two surveys by the Roskill Commission Research Team and one by the British Airports Authority.[19]

[16] The assumption that the affected area is a small fraction of the total housing market may be used to support this proposition.

[17] See Frank de Leeuw (1971), pp. 1–10.

[18] In fact since the evidence on price elasticities is derived from rental accommodation it may be suggested that an elasticity of unity does not generate a proper maximum for the surplus of the *owners* who might be thought to be more committed to their property. Such evidence as is available, however, does not suggest that there is a markedly lower price-elasticity for owners and in particular owner-occupiers. See de Leeuw, *op. cit.*

[19] See *Roskill Reports*, Appendix 23.

The broad conclusions of these surveys was that the surplus revealed in the answers implied that the elasticity was near unity (absolute value).[20] If the price elasticity of the United States applied to English owner-occupiers, the survey suggests values very near to the maximum. One might argue that the evidence (low movement rates in the United Kingdom) is consistent with a lower price elasticity in the U.K. and that the survey does reveal surpluses considerably less than the maximum values. Thus notwithstanding all the many objections which may be levied against a survey technique that asks hypothetical questions, it does not seem that the survey data are inconsistent with what other knowledge is available on the distribution of these surpluses.

THE MEASUREMENT OF D—THE DEPRECIATION IN HOUSE PRICE DUE TO NOISE

The possibility of measuring the depreciation in house prices due to noise nuisance has been questioned by many. For example, it has been argued that an airport gives rise to sustained property- and site-value appreciation relative to other properties—because of job availability and easier access. All property in the vicinity of an airport enjoys capital appreciation at a more rapid rate than property elsewhere. There is little doubt that this is the case. A new airport confers windfall gains on some people—usually knowledgeable speculators. But we are concerned here only with the differential effects due to noise. The issue is to find the rates of relative appreciation of noisy and quiet property.

Fortunately the peculiar geographical incidence of aircraft noise does enable us to observe houses which are similar in terms of access costs to the airport and other centres of employment but which differ dramatically in their experience of aircraft noise. Typically the noise impact is concentrated under the flight paths at either end of the runway; there one will find the noisy houses. But other dwellings roughly the same distance from the airport but not under the flight paths may enjoy an environment virtually free of aircraft noise. We can therefore compare the rate of appreciation of these two houses in order to

[20] For the Roskill Commission survey the implied elasticity (absolute) was 0·96. See J. F. Gautrin (1973).

find the valuation that the market puts on environmental quiet. In practice it is clearly necessary to distinguish according to the degree of noise nuisance as measured by one of indices[21] such as the NNI. Variations in NNI for a given accessibility therefore should give rise to variations in the degree of appreciation.[22]

NON-RESIDENTIAL NOISE COSTS

One of the important questions for the total evaluation of noise is whether the costs we have so far identified—which include the residential noise suffered, the movement costs of those who shift because of noise, etc.—are sufficient to comprehend the total effects of noise. Superficially it seems that something must be added for non-residential noise such as that which is inflicted on schools, hospitals, and other institutions. The Roskill Commission certainly took this view and this attitude was not challenged at any of the public hearings, so one might suppose that there is virtual unanimity of this point. But there is an opposing view which ought to be set out. It may be claimed that the prices of property in a particular area will necessarily reflect all the goods and bads of that district. Thus if there are schools subject to noise in the district the prices of houses will reflect the inferior education which is to be expected there. Furthermore, one would anticipate that there would be a natural selection of those people who do not much care, or need to care, about the educational qualities of the schools. Much the same argument applies to other institutions such as hospitals.

If local hospitals and schools were private enterprise organizations, then the services that they supply would reflect the higher costs of educating or curing and so the additional costs would be reflected in the rents or prices of houses. But such services are not usually organized on private enterprise lines— nor are they wholly or even mainly financed by local taxes. In both schools and hospitals the State plays an important role. The State may finance the sound-proofing of schools and

---

[21] See ch. 2 for a discussion of these measures.

[22] The reader may observe that with noise measurement we have advantages over those who analyse pollution. Access costs and pollution probably vary inversely over the whole range of the sample data.

hospitals—or the closure and reprovision as in the case of the United Kingdom—so that a substantial fraction of the cost is borne by the body of taxpayers as a whole. Any residual deleterious effect—such as a fall in standard of education or health—will be necessarily reflected in the reduced rents and house prices.

It seems sensible therefore to follow the Roskill Commission's approach and make a separate addition to the noise costs due to the non-residential elements. The other question is whether we need to take additional account of the noise disamenity suffered by visitors. At first sight again this seems an obvious issue, but one must speculate that in the case of holiday visitors their disamenity is already reflected in the reductions of rents and residential prices in the noisy areas. Rents and room rates at hotels will reflect either the costs of insulation or the disamenity of noise.

One may object—as indeed many have—that the reduction in rents of houses and hotels in noisy areas does not tell the whole story. This is true. If an amenity such as a free park is very widely used by people from afar then the effect on the reductions in rents may also be spread over a considerable radius. Measurements which are restricted to the noisy areas will much understate the effect.

To carry the argument even further, cannot one attribute some loss to those people who do not use the amenity and have no intention of doing so? We exclude from this category those who 'might' use it or who have a finite probability of enjoying the amenity. There is of course a philanthropic reason why the non-users should be prepared to pay to prevent the noise being inflicted on the amenity; many people willingly pay for things that accrue to other proximate beneficiaries. In principle one should include the philanthropic demand for quiet (for others) in the evaluation of noise. (It is, however, a moot point whether one should not also include the misanthropic demand for noise as well!) The measurement of such a demand, however, is all but impossible and we shall ignore it for the rest of this book.

CONCLUDING REMARKS

One of the continuing problems of economics is that one cannot isolate phenomena in laboratory experiments in order to confront theory with empirical evidence. We must glean evidence when and wherever we can from the actual workings of the market. The important question is to discover the relationship between observed data and the theoretical magnitudes. There is no quick and simple one-to-one correspondence since the data are taken from a dynamic context where many adjustments are taking place whereas the theoretical model abstracts from these effects.

Two major weaknesses in our approach have been exposed. First, we know very little about the search and transactions costs in the market. Their size and how they affect the approach to equilibrium are both observed. Secondly, and perhaps most important, we have only put forward the most rudimentary system of dynamic adjustment, and there is no suggestion that we can measure the speed of adaptation to a new noise source. In particular we cannot plot the effects of uncertainty and partial information on the course of prices and costs.

Nevertheless, there is a sufficient basis for us to approach the available data and see if the theoretical effects do appear. This is the job in chapter 6.

APPENDIX: A NOTE ON THE JOINT DENSITY DISTRIBUTION OF N, D, R, AND S FOR GIVEN NNI

So far we have not been explicit about the distribution of the variables that enter into any noise model and how they are related. One of the lynchpins of the whole distribution is the house price. This we may take as an approximation to the permanent income of the household concerned.[23] For any given price of house we shall suppose that there is a uniform depreciation for a given level of noise: all suffer alike.

The next step is to relate the amount which people will be willing to pay to avoid the noise (LDS), or the amount which people would be just willing to accept in compensation for the noise (HDS), to the levels of permanent income and so, at the second stage, to the house depreciation data. In Figure 5.4 we illustrate the relationship supposed between the distribution of people according to their evaluation of noise (or quiet) and their permanent income or the price of the house that they own. The density distribution for the three values of houses is superimposed in the third dimension and labelled f (high-priced), f (medium-priced), and f (low-priced).

Two interpretations of this figure are possible. First if we assume that movement costs and surplus are zero then the distribution about the mean value, for a given house price, represents the equilibrium adjustment of households to their particular noise taste coefficient. Thus a household observed in the higher part of the medium-house-price distribution would be spending more than the average on quiet. This household would be located in a low-NNI area. With this interpretation of the distribution—corresponding to the theoretical model of chapters 4 and 5—one must note that the shape of the distributions would be skewed to the right.

The second interpretation is that even for a given NNI there will be a distribution of noise sensitivity (or taste coefficient) since no perfect adjustment takes place; people are constrained by movement costs and by the surplus valuation of their house

---

[23] In principle it is convenient to assume that there is perfect correlation between the price of the house and the level of permanent income.

and district. Thus there is a distribution of households with
respect to their noise valuation even though they are all in the
same NNI and so buy the same quantity of quiet.

Reality, of course, undoubtedly lies between these two
interpretations—and we do not know exactly where. Evidence
from McKennell's survey around Heathrow suggested that
much of the distribution was of the second type. There was a
large variation in noise sensitivity within a given NNI. But
these data were collected during the early years of the jet age.
One would expect that the second type of distribution has much
contracted over time; but unfortunately, the latter surveys
such as that around Heathrow in 1967 were not designed to
illuminate this issue.

In the application of the Roskill Noise Cost Model it is
normally considered that the new noise source will impinge
on an area which has hitherto been quiet and so probably
contains more than an average number of perturbables. Thus
the line TT' of Figure 5.4 cannot be independent of the locality.
Those who live in rural peace are likely to worry a lot about
noise and the line TT' would be higher on the valuation scale.
As people adjust to the new source of noise in a hitherto quiet
area, by moving out and being replaced by relatively imperturbable households, the distribution will shift lower down the
valuation-of-noise scale, that is to the left in the figure.

We note one other important feature of this distribution—
the average valuation of noise increases more rapidly than
permanent income. This is then consistent with the finding—
which is adduced in chapter 6—that the permanent income
elasticity of demand for quiet is about 1·7 to 2·0. As incomes
increase people are willing on the average to spend a larger
fraction of their income on a quiet life. Thus the locus TT' is a
curve the slope of which diminishes as we increase income.

Using again the accommodating assumption that permanent
income and house prices are proportional, we can plot the
distribution of the differential surpluses and removal costs
against the level of permanent income (or the value of the
house). The differential surplus will have a distribution about
some mean non-zero value. It is also not only conceivable but
virtually certain that some surpluses will be *negative*—some
people will be quite happy to move if they are reimbursed for

even part of their moving costs. But considering the distribution of the differential surplus and moving costs together, it necessarily follows that the sum cannot be negative except in the very short-run disequilibrium situation, otherwise the householder would already have moved. It is difficult to find any *a priori* reason or any convincing evidence for supposing that the regression curve of $S+R$ on permanent income will

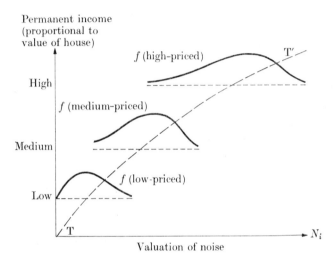

FIG. 5.4. Joint distribution of N_i and permanent income.

have any particular shape such as that shown in Figure 5.5. There is no reason why the degree of attachment to a house should increase more than proportionately to the value of the house. Similarly there is no reason why movement costs should increase more than proportionately with income; normally one would expect the value of time spent in search and settling to increase proportionately with income, and the householder would have an incentive to search while the marginal pay-off in house suitability was expected to exceed his valuation of the time and resources so spent. Consequently, we have shown the regression relation as a line through the origin—but with a cut-off at some minimum value of permanent income. (Also we specify a maximum value for $S+R$ as shown.) The distribution in the above figure for $S+R$ is valid for all NNI. In other words we do not suppose that the relative attachment to a particular property or the moving costs vary because they happen to lie in a noisy or quiet zone.[24] The assumption that the joint distribution of N and $S+R$ is such that D and $S+R$ are

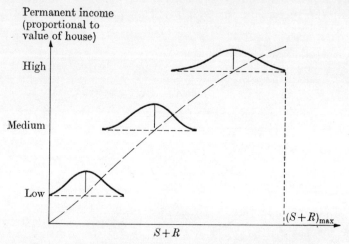

FIG. 5.5. Joint distribution of $(S+R)$ for any NNI

independently distributed makes it particularly easy to form the addition $D+S+R$ and to plot its joint distribution with the value of house (permanent income).

[24] Note that the S value does *not* include the valuation of quiet. However, the question may reasonably be put: "Is there not a strong positive correlation between S and N other than that part of the positive correlation explained by permanent income?" Clearly there is likely to be some such correlation. The observed D (depreciation) on the market is a function of market demand forces emanating from individuals' evaluations of S, R, and N for given fractions of noisy and quiet houses. But high Ss associated with high Ns will offset one another in the adjustment process and so may give rise to the same Ds for any given fraction of quiet/noisy houses. Little can be done about this relationship, however, since we have the greatest difficulty in observing N and S. There is, however, some fragmentary evidence in the testimony and surveys carried out on behalf of the British Airports Authority that N and S are not highly correlated when income (house price) effects are eliminated. (See Roskill Commission (1970b), Documents 5006A and C, and the evidence of Mr. S. P. C. Plowden quoted above.) But this is only a straw. The simplifications introduced by the assumption of zero partial correlation are, however, quite enormous and until evidence is produced to the contrary we shall carry it throughout this discussion.

For a given value of house, therefore, we can plot the distribution of N and $S+D+R$ on the assumption that the two variables are uncorrelated. We then find the fraction of the total frequency in the interval where $N > S+R+D$, and this predicts the number of movers in that house-price category.

CHAPTER 6

Empirical Evidence

EMPIRICAL STUDIES REVIEWED

MANY studies have been carried out on the importance of the various determinants of house prices. Clearly the main factors to be examined are amenity—including aircraft and perhaps other noise—and access. The difficulties experienced in completing such studies are (1) the availability of suitable data, and (2) the elimination of "nuisance variables" to isolate the effect which one means to examine. The availability of data is particularly poor in those countries where by legislation the private citizen and corporation are guaranteed that evidence on the price of a sale although submitted to government for tax purposes will not be disclosed to anyone. This is the case in the United Kingdom where even departments other than the Inland Revenue have no access to these figures. In those circumstances where the true market price of property is thought to be a valuable commercial secret there will be difficulties in obtaining reliable data. One is therefore driven to unofficial and less reliable sources. (The greater abundance of data in the United States suggests that there is much less reticence in revealing prices, and throws much doubt on the supposed widespread desire for confidentiality in the United Kingdom.)

The elimination of "nuisance variables" presents problems since one needs to have a large number of observations in order to isolate significantly the effect of aircraft noise. Perhaps the biggest single "nuisance variable" is the fact that during the general inflation that has accompanied the jet age, all prices have increased and house prices have moved ahead at rates higher than prices in general. Indeed in areas where jet airports have been located the rate of appreciation of houses has been greater than in other areas, on the average. One must therefore study *relative* rates of appreciation. This has been the general approach of most studies. The nature of other nuisance variables depends on the structure of the sample.

The sampling procedures fall into two broad classes—first there are one or two studies that have taken more or less classical random samples, perhaps stratified by house price. This is, however, an unusual approach. The normal method has been to *select* matched samples of houses in a quiet and a noisy environment and to compare rates of appreciation over the critical periods. The main problems with this approach are first to secure a sufficiently large number of observations where there have been two sales during the period of study, and secondly to ensure that the samples really are matched in every possible respect. With all studies there is the problem of houses changing their character by new additions, the personalization of property, and by delapidations.[1] Furthermore, the observed sale prices reflect the value of sound insulation that may have been installed by the previous owner.[2]

The findings of all these studies are mixed. Several of the studies have failed to discover any substantive evidence of differential depreciation due to noise—notwithstanding any claims made to the contrary (by Paik for example). The general reasons for this failure to detect any difference between the price appreciation of noisy and quiet property are (a) faults in the design in the inquiry—and in particular failure to take into account the various nuisance variables which have swamped the results; (b) the failure to match samples in an appropriate way; and (c) a reliance on "appraisers". We can briefly review the main studies on house prices.

McClure (1969). Real-estate data on sales of single family houses between 1955 and 1967 were analysed for three areas near Los Angeles Airport (LAX) and one area (IV) about 10 miles away. McClure measured Pndb and the annual percentage increase in the price of houses over this period. The results are in Table 6.1. McClure adduces from this data and from a subsample which excluded those houses with a more than 20 per cent mean annual change in price that the survey "provides

---

[1] Many of these problems are discussed in detail in Emerson (1970).

[2] This is one reason for supposing that the observed differences have a downward bias in measuring the value of noise.

TABLE 6.1

House prices and noise in Los Angeles 1955–1967

Area	Noise	Average annual percentage increase in price	Stated error
I	95–100 PndB	6·861	0·759
II	90–95	7·639	0·742
III	Some jet noise but less than 90	6·702	0·774
IV	No jet aircraft noises at all	10·121	1·317

no meaningful conclusions about the effects of jet noise on the value of real estate".[3]

McClure's conclusion must be revised for the following reasons:

(1) The Pndb measure is too crude for comparative purposes, and some account should be taken of the number of aircraft heard (as in virtually all composite measures of noise nuisance).

(2) Area III might well be regarded as subject to considerable noise nuisance—for example, if the number of airplanes heard were 200 per day the NNI would be 45 and the CNR would be about 115 indicating that individuals would complain, perhaps vigorously. Thus it is likely that much of area III should be classified as noisy rather than quiet.

(3) With area III so classified, one would adduce from these data that there *is* a difference between the rates of appreciation in the noisy and quiet areas. The best estimate suggests that the difference between the rates of appreciation is of the order of

[3] The argument for excluding from the analysis those residences which have appreciated at more than 20 per cent per annum was that substantial changes would have been made in the property so that one was not comparing like with like. But as McClure points out this gives rise to important biases in interpreting the results—see pp. 16–17. We therefore prefer to rely on the complete sample with the implicit supposition that such major improvements have had more or less the same incidence in all areas. This assumption may give some bias in the opposite direction—but McClure gives some qualitative evidence to the contrary on p. 15.

2½–3 per cent per annum. However, there may be some upward bias in this figure because of the reasons discussed above. But it will be noted that even if one takes a conservative estimate of only 1·5 per cent difference, when applied over 12 years the difference in the selling prices of noisy and quiet houses would be of the order of 20 per cent of the value of the quiet houses.

It is likely that had McClure's data been analysed in an appropriate way the noise depreciation would have been revealed and would not have been "not significant" in the statistical sense. With many reservations and a large margin of error, one may take it that noisy houses will be at something like a 20 per cent discount on quiet houses—but unfortunately little confidence can be placed in this numerical result.

Paik (1970). Paik carried out a cross-section study of residential property values around Kennedy International Airport using housing data from the 1960 census and noise classifications from the 1965 NEF contours. The census uses "self-appraisal" data on house prices and Paik used the median values for blocks. Some four or five measures of the average or mean quality of housing in the blocks were used in order to isolate the NEF effect. The survey showed that there was a statistically significant effect of NEF on the price of the house—roughly, a unit increase in NEF (equal to 1·34 units CNR) gives rise to a decrease in value of $360 of the average house. (Thus one unit change in CNR gives rise to a change of *circa* $270.) Paik did not report the average value of single-family dwellings in the sample. If we suppose that the value is about $25,000 then it implies a 10 per cent depreciation per 10 points change in the CNR (or 7 points in NEF or 15 points NNI).

It is difficult to discover the exact nature of this inquiry (including even the units of measurement) because little is disclosed in the published version. The methodological difficulties of using data of this form are also well known—especially the problem of the split between residential and commercial property use, the issue of "self-appraisal", the use of mean values, and the relatively small number of classificatory variables. The results, however, give higher values for noise effects than do other studies of cities in the United States—for example Emerson's study of Minneapolis (reviewed below) suggests that a ten-unit increase in CNR is associated with

7

only a 4 or 5 per cent depreciation in the value of a house. In
fact the Paik figures are even rather higher than those derived
from all but the high-priced houses (over $24,000 or £10,000)
in the Heathrow survey. But we must also note that 1960, the
year for which the house value data were available, saw the first
surge of jet operation, and consequently the values may reflect
the jet-shock effect (see Crowley below).

Because of the difficulties referred to above it would be
unwise to place much faith in the precise figures. But taken in
conjunction with the other studies Paik's results can be seen
to be broadly consistent although on the high side. As we shall
see below (Dygert and Sanders), the method used by Paik has
been refined and used on a more extensive basis.

Colman (1972). The city of Englewood, California is covered
by 21 census tracts and Colman analysed these tracts according
to the PndB and estimated residential land values based on
'county assessors' data. The PndB ranged from a low of 70 to
a maximum of 113 and the residential land values per square
foot from $2·0 to $3·70, with a mean value of $2·83. The regres-
sion of land value on PndB was:

Land value ($ per square foot) = 5·02 − 0·04(PndB)
where
$$R = 0·549$$

$$t = 2·708$$

$$\text{d.f.} = 17$$

These data therefore imply that for a unit increase in the PndB
the value falls approximately 0·9 per cent (i.e. 0·024/2·83 when
evaluated at the mean value).

Little information is given about the nature of the county
assessor's assessment procedure and we have been unable to
subject it to any consistency tests.[4] The PndB measures are too
crude for the purpose of measuring aircraft noise nuisance (see
comment on McClure above). If we make some allowance for
the effect of number of aircraft heard we would find that the
NNI scale spanned a rather smaller range than the PndB scale,

[4] California law requires that assessments be equal to 25 per cent of market
value. Since the mean residential land value in Englewood is about 5 or 6
times the assessed value in San Mateo (see review of Dygert and Sanders
below) I assume that Colman has used appropriate market values.

since houses slightly to the side of the flight path will hear roughly the same number of aircraft but at a lower PndB. Furthermore, the data include some observations of 70 PbdB reflecting probably the ambient noise level in the area.[5] The errors involved in using a PndB measure to gauge the noise nuisance suggest therefore that there will be also an 'errors in variables' effect on the regression estimate which will cause it to be lower in absolute value than the true value.

There are no data on which we can amend the results for the 'errors in variable' bias, but we can make some adjustments by rescaling the PndB to approximate NNI by increasing the coefficient by 50 per cent. These adjustments suggest that the depreciation is 0·7 per cent per unit NNI. It is likely, however, that the true value is somewhat higher than this.

The rather skimpy nature of the Colman account of the study prevents one putting any great weight on the results of the inquiry—and in particular the lack of corroborative evidence on the assessor's methods inhibits subtle interpretations of the results. One may conjecture that since the houses all fall within the same jurisdiction the assessor's values were at least consistent with market values—that is to say they would constitute the same fraction of market price throughout the area. It will be observed that the noise variable explained about 30 per cent of the variation in values. Such a high percentage of the variance explained may testify to the otherwise homogeneous nature of the community at Englewood. One would therefore accept the Englewood data as contributory evidence on the effects of noise, but one should place only a modest degree of confidence in the numerical results.

Crowley (1972). Four sample areas were selected—one adjacent to Toronto International Airport in the western suburbs and two others which were located at roughly the same distance from the central business district (C.B.D.) but in the eastern suburbs. The areas were chosen as matched samples so that they were as comparable as possible in terms of "population density, age of housing", and presumably other socio-economic factors. The main findings were that (1) there was no clear difference between the level of residential land prices in the airport area and the two control areas, and inter-area

[5] This "flattens" the regression at the low PndB values.

variation in house prices was not explained by the airport, and
(2) residential land values in the airport area fall during periods
of "shock", that is when there is a dramatic change in the
intensity of use of runways or when jets make their debut in
large numbers, but rise again to a trend similar to that in the
control areas. The author explains this shock period results in
terms of the many changes in land use that are induced during
the shock period.

Perhaps the main weakness in this study is the fact that the
matching process did not take account of the value of the airport and surrounding industry as a source of employment. (The
author does, however, refer to the westward drift of Toronto.)
Such proximity to the airport employment source may at least
compensate and perhaps overcompensate for the deleterious
effects of noise on residential property.[6] Unfortunately, the
author did not collect data for a control area near the airport
but in a quiet zone so there is no possibility of checking this
conjecture.

Although the design of the study did not enable the author
properly to measure the differential effects of aircraft noise on
house prices, the results are very useful in describing the time
series of house prices in the various adjustment periods. Furthermore, Crowley provides useful data on turnover rates to which
we shall return.

Emerson (1969). Emerson analysed a cross-section of 222
sales of single-family houses in 1967. The author set out to
determine the many factors that influenced the price—including
aircraft noise as measured by the CNR (in steps of 5 from 100
to 125). Using 26 independent variables the author analysed the
the determinants of the price of houses. The results (Table 6.2)
show that there was evidence of a noise depreciation effect.

This is the most sophisticated and comprehensive study so
far carried out in the United States. It seems very likely that it
has substantially isolated the effect of aircraft noise, and there
is a significant difference in the case of the highest noise levels.
Furthermore, Emerson has avoided some of the pitfalls of the

---

[6] To indicate orders of magnitude suppose that location near the airport
reduces the average expected commuting distance per household by 5 miles;
then at 10 cents a mile the annual saving will be of the order of $2,500—
probably of the order of 5–10 per cent per house. This is of the same order as
other figures for depreciation due to noise.

time-series analysis of changes in prices which may well reflect merely changes in other conditions (such as freeway access, differential pollution etc.). The noise depreciation reported by Emerson seems to be relatively low when compared with those for Los Angeles or even for the United Kingdom (London). This may be explained in part at least by the fact that Minneapolis has an extreme climate and for most of the year closed

TABLE 6.2

House Prices and Minneapolis Airport (1967)

CNR	Percentage depreciation due to noise
115 to 119	2·7
120 to 124	4·6
125 and over	9·6

and sealed windows are the rule with perhaps air-conditioning in summer. In Los Angeles, on the other hand, open-air patio living is common all the year round, and in London open windows and natural ventilation are the rule throughout the year. The greater depreciation in Los Angeles and London compared with Minneapolis may reflect the fact that not being able to open windows is not much of a cost in Minnesota.

One must clearly regard Emerson's estimates as the best available indicators of the effect of aircraft noise on houses prices in the United States. They are not inconsistent with the findings for London and Los Angeles. However, for different values of house, Emerson did *not* show that there was a different rate of depreciation—and this was a characteristic of the London studies.

Dygert and Sanders (1970). This was a cross-section study of San Mateo County in the proximity of San Francisco International Airport. The values of properties as assessed for taxation purposes were the main dependent variable and there were also available data on the area of the plot and buildings. Thus derived variables were used—such as mean land value per square foot—in order to standardize the results. The independent variables were a long list, similar to those considered by

Emerson, that are believed to be significant in determining the value of a property—such as distance to shopping centres, access to freeway and to San Francisco Central Business District. The noise measure was the CNR index.

The basic method of analysis was cross-section regression rather similar to that used by Emerson. The authors interpret their results in terms of the standard statistical tests and find that "in 12 out of the 20 models" aircraft noise was a significant (0·95 level) in determining the value of the property.

One has many interpretations of the results of the study. However, the general effects may be summarised in two forms: (a) for one additional CNR median land value loses $0·0044 to $0·0047 per square foot, (b) for one additional CNR the mean house value loses $109·75 to $113·69.

If we translate the result in (a) into a house depreciation figure on the basis of $\frac{1}{4}$-acre lots and a 1:5 ratio of land to total property value we get a figure of $240·55 per CNR. No doubt there is some under-assessment in (b) which is characteristic of virtually all property tax assessments and this may account for the difference between the (a) and (b) results.

The reliance on data pertaining to the 1960 census, on the one hand, and on the tax assessment of value of property, on on the other, does emphasize the rather fragile basis of the whole exercise—indeed this is fully recognized by the authors. The most important issue is whether the appraised variation in the value due to aircraft noise is an absolute or a relative figure. The authors have interpreted the results as though the absolute figure was the appropriate interpretation and I have followed their example.

The Dygert and Sanders study should be ranked second to that of Emerson in the studies of the United States. The results on land values are remarkably similar to those reviewed above (see Paik, for example) and are rather above those of Emerson. On the other hand the dwelling data fall well within Emerson's range. We conclude therefore that Dygert's results are consistent with those of the other studies.[7]

[7] I am grateful to Dr. Harvey B. Safeer of the Office of Noise Abatement, Dept. of Transportation, Washington D.C., for most useful discussions about Dygert's results and their interpretation.

Roskill (1970). A sample of 20 estate agents (realtors) were asked to compare house-price levels within different areas as specified on a large-scale map of the areas in the vicinity of Heathrow and Gatwick airports. The average values of the responses are shown in Table 6.3. In order to test these data the

TABLE 6.3

Percentage Depreciation of Houses Compared with Houses Outside the 35 NNI Contour (= 95 CNR)

Class of property	35 to 45 NNI	45 to 55 NNI	Over 55 NNI
		HEATHROW	
Low price (Av. £3,000)	0	2·9	5·0
Medium price (Av. £6,000)	2·6	6·3	10·5
High price (Av. £10,000)	3·3	13·3	22·5
		GATWICK	
Low price	4·5	10·3	N/A
Medium price	9·4	16·5	N/A
High price	16·4	29·0	N/A

Roskill Commission Research Team carried out an analysis of actual prices of house transactions to find the relative rates of increase in prices of noisy and quiet property. The sample was chosen so that houses had not undergone any substantial change from the time before the noise to the time after the noise shadow was imposed. Comparability was ensured by the District Valuer of the Inland Revenue service matching the two samples. The results—put out as a Further Research Team Work Paper[8]—were consistent with those reported in the above table. (I must confess that, as a member of the Roskill Commission, I was somewhat surprised by the consistency since I expected that there would be significant biases in the reporting of the estate agents. It is necessary to record that the Director of the Research Team, Mr. Frank Thompson,

[8] Roskill Commission (1970c)

was correct and I was wrong in believing that the results would not be so biased.) Subsequently the figures were publicly examined by the large number of contending parties at the public hearings of the Commission and no serious challenge to their validity was put forward.[9]

Notwithstanding the objections to the use of appraisers' opinions, it seems that one may have some considerable faith in the Roskill results—partly because of the consistency of the appraisers' returns and partly because of the fact that the independent inquiry into actual sales confirmed the survey results.[10] One of the main advantages of the Roskill data is that we have depreciation data for ranges of house prices—and we note that the more expensive the house the greater the *rate* of depreciation. A second feature is that one can compare the depreciation figures for a well-established urban airport, Heathrow, with those for an airport in an essentially rural (commuter belt) location, Gatwick.[11]

Roskill data are the most comprehensive in coverage and have not been discredited by the various tests to which they have been subjected. Although one would like more data on actual sales and a more detailed analysis over time to see how the trends change, we propose in this study to make the best use of what evidence was collected.

VARIOUS LEGAL CASES

In the United Kingdom the history of the legislation on aircraft noise is indeed simple. Section 9(1) of the Air Navigation Act 1920 first denied recourse to the courts for trespass by a

[9] A thorough survey of the material on London has been carried out by J. F. Gautrin (1973). The most remarkable feature is that the many studies carried out with different methodologies and by quite different people all gave rather similar results. This above all gives one reason to believe that the results are not simply the manifestation of a statistical artifact or of a methodological bias.

[10] It ought to be recorded that the British Airports Authority also carried out a postal survey of some 200 estate agents in the south-east of England asking what fall in price they would have expected in houses in 'very noisy' (near 45–50 NNI) and 'noisy' (40–45) areas, and obtained very similar results to those recorded here. See Roskill Commission (1970b), Documents. It is believed other surveys were also carried out but since the results confirmed those above they were not reported.

[11] Heathrow is some 15 miles from Central London, whereas Gatwick is about 30.

nuisance caused by aircraft flying over property. Subsequently the Civil Aviation Act 1949 in Section 40(1) substantially re-enacted the provisions of the 1920 statute. The Airports Authority Act of 1965 made provision for grants for the sound-proofing of dwellings affected by aircraft noise, and the Land Compensation Act of 1973 Part II Sections 20 and 21 extended these arrangements. The 1965 provisions provided for partial compensation for soundproofing but only for houses inside the 55 NNI contour

The broad effect of all this legislation up to 1972 has been to enable the aviation industry to ignore the citizens' reasonable presumption of freedom from jet-noise. Soundproofing grants were restricted, small, and quite inadequate as a means of compensation. There was no recourse to the counts to secure compensation for the suffering caused by aircraft noise. This situation contrasts sharply with that in the United States where there has been no law similar to the Air Navigation Act of the United Kingdom.

The Land Compensation Act of 1973, however, is meant to mark a turning-point in the history of the treatment of compensation. The Act makes it possible for an owner to make a claim against the government for the depreciation that his property has suffered due to 'noise, vibration, smell, fumes, smoke and artificial lighting ...' from public works which include 'any aerodrome' (Part I (2)). The claims are to be made only for new works and they include 'new aprons' and 're-aligned runways' (Part I(9)). No claim can be made for existing nuisances or even a more intensive nuisance such as the greater frequency or heavier and noisier aircraft on an existing runway (Part I(3)). The intention is clearly to restrict compensation only to those injuriously affected by new aprons and newly aligned runways.

Compensation seems to be defined at market value—but there are many difficulties since the valuation clearly depends critically on planning permission and expectations of such permits. The intention of the statute seems to be to take the *ab initio* planning conditions as par. Presumably these various problems of the definition and measurement of compensation will be sorted out in the Lands Tribunal—which appears to be the final court for resolving disputes. It is clear that much

new evidence will need to be collected and interpreted in order
to settle the many issues that will arise. But as experience shows,
in the United States the courts have been rather confused on
these settlements.

In the United States, for more than a quarter of a century,
there has been developing a body of legal opinion on the effects
of airport noise on the value of real property. A U.S. Supreme
Court case of 1946, *United States* v. *Causby*,[12] marked the
beginning of this development, which Michael Berger has
called "one of the most tangled chapters in American legal
history".[13]

In the *Causby* case, the Court found that direct over-flights
of low-flying propellor aircraft had depreciated the value of a
chicken farm owned by the plaintiffs. The court asserted that a
"taking" of the property had occurred because the flights were
"so low and frequent as to be a direct and immediate interference with the enjoyment and use of the land".[14]

Subsequent to the *Causby* decision, questions were raised in
various state and federal courts concerning such matters as:
the agency to be held responsible for the damages if awarded;[15]
the requirement that the offending flights be directly over the
property damaged;[16] whether the "taking" must be total or
merely partial;[17] and so on.

By 1966 a rather firm rule about compensation of noise
sufferers was being followed by most, if not all, courts. As
stated by an Oregon appeals court, this rule requires the
following:

The property test to determine where there has been a compensable
invasion of the individual's property rights in a case of this kind is
where the interference with use and enjoyment is of sufficient
magnitude to support a conclusion that the interference has reduced
the fair market value of the plaintiff's land by a certain sum of
money. If so, justice as between the state and the citizen requires

[12] 328 U.S. 256.
[13] "Nobody Loves an Airport," *So. Cal. Law Review*, vol. 43, no. 4 (Fall
1970), p. 642.
[14] 328 U.S. 256.
[15] *Griggs* v. *County of Allegheny*, 369 U.S. 84 (1962).
[16] *Thornburg* v. *Port of Portland*, 233 Ore. 178, 376 P. 2d 100 (1962).
[17] *Batten* v. *United States*, 306 F. 2d. 580 (10th Cir. 1962).

the burden imposed to be borne by the public and not by the individual alone.[18]

In 1970, in the California Supreme Court, a significant case, *Aaron* v. *City of Los Angeles*,[19] was decided in favour of hundreds of property-owners in the vicinity of Los Angeles International Airport. Plaintiffs numbering 1,500 who owned about 750 parcels of property alleged that:

Noise from jet aircraft flying over and near the residential properties of plaintiffs has resulted in a substantial diminution in the market value of these properties, which thus constitutes a 'taking or damaging' of these properties within the purview of Article I, Section 14 of the California Constitution.[20]

Various appraisers presented testimony in this case concerning changes in market values, "price-trend" studies that had been conducted, etc.[21] The decision commented that the "approach and opinions of plaintiffs' appraisers leave much to be desired"; yet the decision went in favour of the plaintiffs, and from $800 to $6,000 was awarded to each of about 600 property-owners.

The *Aaron* decision relied on Noise Exposure Forecast (NEF) contours for part of its reasoning. NEF contours were accepted by the court as "a good means of drawing a reasonable line between those landowners who may establish a cause of action for inverse condemnation and those who may not".[22] Thus the property-owners inside the 40 NEF contour (approximately the same as CNR 115) became eligible to recover damages but only "to the extent that they are able to establish that jet aircraft noise has diminished substantially the market value of their property."[23]

By no means can the *Aaron* decision be reduced to a formula for computing property damages as a function of some agreed-upon noise measure. But the acceptance of NEF as a valid yardstick may have begun a trend toward quantification of the damage—noise relationship by the courts. It must be admitted, however, that there is a case in which NEF itself has been

[18] *Thornburg* v. *Port of Portland*, 415 P. 2d. 750 (1966).
[19] 11 Avi 17, 642.
[20] Ibid.
[21] Ibid.
[22] Ibid.
[23] Ibid.

belittled. This was *Virginians for Dulles* v. *John Volpe*,[24] decided in May of 1972, in which the NEF measure was attacked by the court as "too imprecise for measuring or even predicting with any degree of accuracy, the environmental impact on the community of aircraft noise or community response to that noise".[25]

In a Connecticut U.S. District Court decision in 1971, *East Haven* v *Eastern*,[26] the problem of awarding damages for airport noise to landowners near the New Haven Airport was actually reduced to a formula. The particular formula employed did not depend on NEF or any other composite noise measure. Instead, it used only factors of location of a parcel of property with respect to the runway of an airport of known amounts of traffic. The formula was adapted from one devised by Thomas H. Hall III and William R. Beaton (1965); it has several weaknesses besides its over-simplicity and has not been used in any other recent case.

Also in 1971, a decision in a California appeals court, *Nestle* v. *City of Santa Monica*,[27] discussed the use of CNR contours with some sympathy, though in the course of a decision denying recovery of damages due to airport noise. Appraisers' testimony on the diminution of property values was cited in what by then had become a standardized format, and the court firmly stated that 'Damages in inverse condemnation are limited to recovery of diminution in the value of property; they do not include recovery for annoyance or emotional stress.'[28]

The *Nestle* case was appealed to the California Supreme Court, where the lower court was upheld in their conclusion that dimunition of market value had not been proved. Moreover, the importance of establishing a link between airport noise and decrease in property values was underscored by the court, as follows: 'It would appear that appellants could not rest solely on even massive and uncontradicted evidence of excessive noise levels occasioned by the use of jet aircraft to

[24] Civil Action No. 507-70-A in the U.S. District Court for the Eastern District of Virginia.
[25] Ibid.
[26] 11 Avi 18, 289.
[27] App 97 Cal Rptr 235.
[28] Ibid.

prove a decrease in property value.'[29] It is interesting that the
California Supreme Court, in this case, gave hope to the plaintiffs that inverse condemnation may not be the only route to
follow. The lower court had barred the plaintiffs from recovery
for alleged nuisance but the higher court reversed this judgment
and said that California law "does not bar nuisance actions
against public entities".[30]

The current state of legal opinion in compensation for airport
noise is one of confusion, despite some of the clear decisions
cited above and partly because of them. Suits abound—
especially in the Los Angeles area—and some airports are
responding by purchasing large tracts of noise-affected land.
Meanwhile the Federal Aviation Administration has withdrawn
NEF as a proposed national standard, and as a result the courts
will have less guidance than expected.

EMPIRICAL EVIDENCE ON THE DEMAND
FOR A QUIET LIFE

We can use the Roskill data to adduce some of the characteristics of the demand for a quiet life. The figures are derived
from a cross-section sample at a particular time. The first task
therefore is to measure the elasticity of demand for quiet with
respect to income. No information is available on the incomes of
sample households in the house-price depreciation data. But
the price of the house in which a family lives is a good indicator
of the level of *permanent income* of that household. Evidence
from studies of housing suggest that the elasticity of demand for
housing with respect to permanent income is of the order of
unity. Thus the value of the house can be used as a cardinal
indicator of the level of permanent income of the household.
The question of the extent of adjustment to noise is a real one.
It seems reasonable to assume that at Heathrow residents were
more or less completely adjusted to the noise pollution; at
Gatwick, however, it is conceivable that some adjustment was
still proceeding. The extent to which this adjustment affects
the rate of depreciation is not known and *faute de mieux* we
assume that no such effects are significant.

---

[29] *Ira Nestle* v. *City of Santa Monica*, Sup. 101 Gal Rptr 568.
[30] Ibid.

From table 6.3 we can adduce a general rule: *a doubling of the permanent income (house price) is associated with a doubling of the percentage of total permanent income spent on quiet.* Or to put it in another form, a twofold increase in income is associated with a fourfold increase in the spending on quiet. The elasticity of demand for a quiet life with respect to permanent income is approximately 2.

This rule seems to correspond very closely to the facts for Heathrow, especially for the well-defined noisy areas over 45 NNI. For Gatwick, however, the elasticity appears to be somewhat lower than 2—probably 1·7 is the best representative figure. But in any case it is reasonably clear that a quiet life is a luxury good—the percentage spent thereon expands between 70 per cent and 100 per cent more rapidly than income.

One must pause and ask, however, whether such a cross-section result can be interpreted in a time-series sense. For example, can one predict that a 3 per cent growth in income *per capita* will be associated with a 5¼–6 per cent increase in spending on quiet? This is a proper conclusion provided that the relative price of quiet does not change. First, it may be objected that such an assumption cannot be correct since the growth of population and incomes will almost certainly increase the relative scarcity of quiet. One ought properly to take into account the rising trend in the price of quiet and the substitution of other goods and services. There is also a second objection to such a time-series interpretation of the cross-section results. Observations at a moment of time reflect the *relative* social values of that time and it is by no means clear that today the middle class will behave in twenty years time as the upper middle class do today. However, data from cross-section studies, when properly interpreted in a permanent income sense, have performed reasonably well in predicting time series —and that is after all the acid test. In the absence of convincing rebuttal evidence, therefore, we shall interpret the cross-section results as though they are valid also in a time-series extrapolation.

We can now compare the different figures for Gatwick and Heathrow and attempt to account for the difference. One might presume at first that the differences could be explained by the fact that with separate housing markets in Sussex and Surrey

(Gatwick) and around Heathrow, the relative scarcity of quiet houses was much greater in Sussex than around Heathrow. This would mean that at Gatwick the price of noisy houses must be reduced more than at Heathrow because there were relatively more of them to be occupied and owned. But if our Cobb–Douglas assumption that the elasticity of demand for quiet is (minus) unity were true,[31] then such a differential supply and relatively high price of quiet in Gatwick would not give rise to any variation in the *expenditure* on quiet for any given income group.[32] It seems therefore as though one may superficially interpret the difference in expenditures on quiet for given NNI as evidence which discredits the unit elasticity assumption; indeed if one could show that the area around Gatwick contained relatively more noisy houses than London's Heathrow area, one would be able to claim this as evidence of the *inelasticity* of demand for quiet.

Such an inference would not be justified for the following reasons. (1) Since the area around Gatwick is rural in character the ambient background noise is some 6 PbdB less than that in the area around the airport at Heathrow. Consequently, the same NNI is more intrusive in the Gatwick area than in the Heathrow area. Using the NNI scale one would therefore regard 45 NNI at Heathrow as approximately equivalent to 39 NNI at Gatwick.[33] This adjustment clearly goes a considerable way toward explaining the figures—on the average it accounts for some 60–70 per cent of the difference.[34]

(2) The relative depreciation rates of houses reflect not merely the current conditions as measured in the NNI but primarily expectations of future growth, and the rate of growth of traffic at Gatwick was clearly expected to be much greater than that

[31] Note that a Cobb–Douglas form is sufficient but not necessary for a unit elasticity of demand.

[32] This conclusion assumes that the people at Gatwick and Heathrow have the same taste coefficient (b_i in chapters 4 and 5 above). We examine whether this is a reasonable presumption below.

[33] This does assume that 1 PndB of other noise is the same as one of aircraft noise.

[34] To put the matter another way, when one buys a house in the Gatwick area one normally incurs large expenses in commuting cost for the advantage of a peaceful home environment. If that peace is destroyed by aircraft then the advantages of the Gatwick area are very seriously impaired—much more so than if the same noisy aircraft were imposed on the already noisy West London.

at Heathrow. If one assumed that the rate of growth of movements at Gatwick to 1975 were roughly twice Heathrow, one would account for about two to three points of the NNI scale.[35] (3) A further technical factor suggests that NNI in Gatwick is more burdensome than NNI at Heathrow. The NNI does not take into account the noise made by night operations—and these were relatively much more frequent at Gatwick than at Heathrow, where there were restrictions on night flights movements. Movements at night are much more (10 times) of a nuisance than day operations.

All these considerations therefore suggest that, were an appropriate measure for the noise nuisance to be used, there would be no dramatic difference in the Gatwick and Heathrow figures. In particular it cannot be adduced from these data that there is an inelastic demand for quiet. The data are broadly consistent with a unit elasticity of demand—but conversely one cannot claim that such a hypothesis has been critically tested with such figures. More direct evidence is required on the price elasticity of demand for quiet.

Let us return to the finding that the permanent income elasticity of demand for quiet is of the order of 1·7–2·0. It would be useful if there were corroborative evidence of this result. At first sight it appears that Emerson is reporting evidence of this kind for Minneapolis when he says (p. 83): "… the noise nuisance variable proved to be systematically more statistically significant as a determinant of price as one moves from lower to higher-valued segments (i.e. higher valued houses), an income inelasticity of demand for freedom from aircraft nuisance which rises with income is implied." This conclusion is drawn from the data of table 6.4, where the percentages indicate the depreciation due to noise as derived from the cross-section regression coefficients for three "segments" of the housing market—low-, medium-, and high-priced. Clearly the conclusion that the income elasticity increases as incomes rise is not implied either by the estimates of the table or by the level of significance associated with them. The estimates themselves suggest that the percentage depreciation goes *down* as the value

---

[35] This is a guess only. To do the job properly would require extensive calculations of the expected noise disbenefit duly discounted to find present value.

Table 6.4

Emerson's Predictions from Cross-Section Regression

Composite Noise rating	Low value $P = \$14,412$	Medium value $P = \$18,835$	High value $P = \$25,848$	Full sample $P = \$19,683$
100	0	0	0	0
105	0.98% $141	?	0.87% $255	0.81% $159
110	2.7% $389	0.08% $15	2.0% $517	1.6% $319
115	4.9% $713	0.18% $34	3.4% $879	2.7% $531
120	8.5% $1.226	0.24% $45	5.8% $1,499	4.6% $905
125	18.2% $2,628	0.49% $92	12.5% $3,231	9.8% $1,935
Level of significance:	0.75+	0.84+	0.85+	0.90+

Source: Emerson (1969), p. 83.

of the house increases—if we compare only the low and high values. But a really curious feature of the estimates is the very low, indeed virtually zero, percentages of depreciation found for the medium-priced houses. Emerson does not mention this fact or attempt to explain it, except with respect to the rather large pseudo-sampling errors. Without access to the original data it is difficult to explore these effects any further. It is clear, however, that the fact that the nuisance variable became "statistically more significant" the higher the value of a house implies nothing whatsoever about the direction of change of the value of the best numerical estimate of the depreciation figure.[36] The only implication of lower relative standard errors is that the best estimates, whatever their numerical value, have a smaller confidence interval. In ordinary language our confidence in the estimate, whatever it is, increases as the relative

[36] It is difficult to give any logical meaning to "statistically more significant"—either an estimate is or is not significantly different from the null hypothesis for a given probability level. Emerson seems to use this phrase to mean that the relative standard errors of the estimates decrease as the value of houses increases.

standard error declines. If for example we compare the high-
and low-priced houses we would adduce that the permanent
income elasticity of demand for quiet was *less* than unity (that
is residential quiet is a "necessity") and would use the two
standard errors to give an indication of the confidence one
placed in such a finding.

One must conclude that the findings of Emerson do not
support his assertion of "increasing income elasticity of
demand".[37] The standard errors are such that any difference
between the subsamples of low-, medium-, and high-price
property would easily have arisen from chance, and so we can
adduce no conclusion about the income elasticity of demand.

We may tentatively conclude as follows:

(1) There is evidence that houses suffering from aircraft noise
experience a depreciation in their price relative to quiet houses.
Those studies that have failed to find an aircraft noise effect
have normally failed to standardize for the many other variables
and attributes that affect the price which a house will command
on the market.

(2) There is some tentative evidence that the elasticity of
demand for residential quiet is of the order of 2 indicating that
residential quiet is a luxury good.

(3) Differing rates of depreciation due to noise may be due to a
variation in the relative supply of noisy/quiet houses, but we
are able to explain the differential between Gatwick and
Heathrow by other aspects of the neighbourhoods and so we
cannot use the changed-relative-supply-same-demand hypothesis in order to measure the price elasticity of the demand for
residential quiet.

SUMMARY OF EMPIRICAL FINDINGS ON
NOISE DEPRECIATION

One convenient way to represent the findings on noise
depreciation is to use the following measure:

$$\text{Noise Depreciation Sensitivity Index (NDSI)} = \frac{\text{Difference in percentage depreciation}}{\text{Difference in noise rating (NNI or CNR or NEF)}}.$$

---

[37] I assume also that Emerson means the less restrictive and somewhat
different condition of "*high* income elasticity of demand," i.e. an elasticity
exceeding unity.

For example, in the NNI index we have the obvious mnemonic:

$$\text{NDSI(NNI)} = \frac{\Delta D}{\Delta \text{NNI}},$$

and we shall normally interpret the NDSI as positive. This measures the noise sensitivity of the housing market in terms of the percentage discount reactions to a unit (NNI) change in noise. The results of the various studies are summarized in NDSI(NNI) terms in Table 6.5.

TABLE 6.5

NDSI(NNI)

Study	Location	NDSI	Confidence	Comments
McClure	Los Angeles	0.7	Very low	Difficult to guess CNR and NNI from PndB. Inappropriate analysis of data.
Colman	Los Angeles	0.7	Fair	Little information on values and method of valuation.
Paik	N.Y. Kennedy	0.7	Low	Methodological problems of self-assessment and standards.
Emerson	Minneapolis	0.4	High	Note climatic extremes. The NDSI also *increases* with the noise level.
Dygert and Sanders	San Francisco	0.3 to 0.7	Fairly High	Much depends on the validity of using 1960 data for 1970 noise.
Roskill	Heathrow (London)	0i4 1.0	Moderate	The basis for these figures is at least two estate agents' surveys, and an analysis of house prices; both levels and rate of increases in 1960s NDSIs are *constant* as noise level increases.
	Gatwick (London)	0.7		

(In order to convert these values to NDSI(CNR) we would simply add roughly 50 per cent.)

It will be noted that the NDSI may be equated to the ratio of the price of quiet to the price of the house. Thus if P_h is the price of the 'basic house' and q_2 is the amount of quiet corresponding to NNI $= x$ and q_1 the amount of quiet corresponding to NNI $= x-1$, then the NDSI is:

$$\frac{100(Pq_2 - Pq_1)/P_h}{q_2 - q_1} = 100\,\frac{P}{P_h}.$$

where P is the price of quiet which is held constant across the cross-section. Units of quiet are measured in equivalent NNI terms. To put the NDSI on a standard basis, therefore, we can calculate what the price of quiet would be for a given value of house. In the Roskill evidence we note that the NDSI changes dramatically for a change in the value of the house. In Table 6.6 we show the average values of house from which the NDSIs were calculated. It is clear that Emerson's average house values for Minneapolis are below those of McClure and those of the

TABLE 6.6

Study	NDSI	Average price of house	NDSI(NNI) adjusted for price of house (standard $25,000)
McClure	0·7	$25,000+	0·7
Colman	0·7	($27,000?)	0·7
Paik	0·7	not known[38]	0·7
Emerson	0·4	($19,683)	0·55
Dygert and Sanders	0·3–0·7	($21,000)	0·4–0·8
Roskill			
Heathrow	1·0	($25,000)	1·0
Gatwick	1·3	($25,000)	1·3

Notes: Colman's values are guessed from the general knowledge about the noise affected area. McClure reports that houses to be insulated were in the $25,000–30,000 range but he deals with a standard $34,000 house (exchange rate $2·50 for the pound). Dygert and Sanders report that by California law property is assessed at 25 per cent of the appraised market value, so their mean assessment of $7,016 is approximately $28,000 market value.

[38] The area of Paik's study is not revealed, but presumably it was in South Queens and perhaps the Town of Hempstead, possibly including Rockaways. The average dwelling probably cost rather more than our standard $25,000 but there is no way to check this.

high-class houses in the Roskill sample. If therefore we use the variation of the NDSIs with income as it appears in the Roskill data to adjust the Emerson NDSI so that it corresponds to an average house price of $25,000, then the NDSI for Minneapolis must be increased by about 0·15 to 0·2 points. Thus we obtain the final column of adjusted NDSIs in the table above.[39]

Perhaps the most striking feature of this column of adjusted NDSIs is the similarity of the results. For a $25,000 house one pays between 0·4 and 0·7 per cent ($100 to $175) for a unit NNI increase in quiet in the United States. (Corresponding figures for a unit change in CNR are 0·7 and 1·0 per cent and $145 to $250.) Considering that the studies have used a considerable diversity of material, relate to different districts, cover different environments, and have proceeded with rather different methodologies, there is a remarkable consistency in the results. It appears, however, that the London results suggest a higher spending on quiet for the given house value.

CAN NNI OR CNR UNITS BE USED AS CARDINAL ECONOMIC QUANTITIES?

As we saw in the discussion of the quantitative measures of noise nuisance there is no obvious reason why the monotonic variables NNI, CNR, or NEF should correspond to *economic* measures of quantity. The NNI, CNR, and NEF are indicators of ordinal significance for they were constructed on the principle that the less noise—measured as a mixture of frequency and peak intensity—the better. However, it may be that the NNI etc. do in fact correspond to a simple economically valid quantitative measure. The acid test is the correspondence to the facts.

In the cross-section of percentage depreciation for a given value of house at various NNI levels, we can suppose that the observations relate to the same price of quiet—whatever units that quality is measured in. Thus the expenditure on quiet will measure the number of units of quiet multiplied by the constant price per unit of quiet. The unit of measurement is arbitrary. Let us therefore define it as a 1 per cent of the value of the house, so that for a given value of house the actual percentage

---

[39] This amendment may be considered to be inconsistent with Emerson's findings on the income effect. If one rejects the Roskill income-effect and accepts the nul hypothesis then the Minneapolis NDSI remains at 0·4.

depreciation measures the quantity of noise suffered, that is the negative of the quantity of quiet purchased.

It follows, therefore, that for a given value of house, the quantitative measure of noise (or quiet) that is economically meaningful can be found by investigating how the expenditure on quiet varies for different NNIs. One special case is of obvious interest: if the depreciation rates increase *linearly* with NNI over the relevant range then it will follow that the NNI is an economically meaningful measure of quantity—with an arbitrary unit of measurement. In principle one should also be able to extrapolate and find a true economic zero-noise or maximum-quiet point.

TABLE 6.7

	Change in percentage depreciation	
	40 to 50 NNI	50 to 60 NNI
Low-price house	2·9	2·1
Medium-price house	3·7	4·2
High-price house	10·0	9·2

Note: These increases are biased upwards because the depreciation at 40 NNI is shown as zero instead of a small positive value.

Now it so happens that the Roskill (Heathrow) data are broadly consistent with this special linear relationship. If we record the increase in the percentage depreciation and the increase in the mid-point of the NNI range we get the results shown in Table 6.7. We may interpret these results to indicate that the two sets of figures are sufficiently close to one another to suggest that the linear hypothesis cannot be rejected. An increase in one unit NNI induces the same change in the percentage depreciation, whatever the level of the NNI may happen to be. These data also suggest that the zero point for Heathrow should be about 36.[40]

[40] Unfortunately, we cannot use the Gatwick data to check this hypothesis since there are no observations over 55 NNI. We can, however, use the linear hypothesis to find a zero for Gatwick and it turns out to be in the region 28 to 30.

Obviously the linear hypothesis with respect to NNI, CNR, or NEF is an extremely simple and useful one. Until such a time as it is convincingly discredited by the data it seems worth-while retaining it. However, it may appear that the data collected by Emerson can be taken as discrediting the linear hypothesis. The diagram showing the percentage depreciation and the CNR for Emerson's statistics exhibits a remarkable non-linearity—increasing with CNR at an increasing rate. However, we cannot accept this relationship as evidence from the data. In fact Emerson *assumed* that 'the effects of the nuisance or property values increases, *ceteris paribus*, at an increasing rate with the level of nuisance, possibly significantly only above a threshold level of aircraft nuisance' (p. 66). And so his results were constrained to satisfy this assumption; consequently one cannot adduce any evidence bearing on the linearity hypothesis from Emerson's calculations.[41]

We tentatively conclude therefore that the linear hypothesis is not discredited by the data at present available. It must be emphasized, however, that little faith should be vested in this result until it has undergone more stringent and extensive tests. But the simplicity of the tentative hypothesis is clearly attractive and useful for quick calculations.

MOVEMENT RATES AND NOISE

Theoretically one of the effects of putting a new source of airport noise on a community would appear in the turnover rates of houses. One would predict that sensitive persons will move out of and imperturbables will move into the affected area. In principle observations of numbers of movement should enable one to calibrate the distribution of households by their valuation of noise sensitivity—as we have specified it in chapter 5. In practice there are many difficulties that prevent such a study from being undertaken. First, internal migration data are generally scarce and often unreliable for intercensus years; and census years are too far apart for useful analysis. Secondly, the definition of a "movement" is not obvious. For example the disintegration of a household through divorce may result in

---

[41] It would be easy to design a test of the linearity hypothesis with the aid of Emerson's data. One could fit a regression with the noise variable measured in CNR terms and compare the goodness-of-fit of the line with the fit with Emerson's transformed variable. But this must be left for later analysis.

two or more households one of which will normally move. Thirdly, even by direct inquiries, it is difficult to find those who have moved "because of the noise". Normally they will be scattered over the quiet areas and will be difficult to detect except by very expensive follow-up techniques. Fourthly, it is normally impossible to distinguish either *ex post* or *ex ante* between those who moved because of the noise and those who moved for other reasons—the so-called "natural movers".

Nevertheless, in spite of the difficulties it would be possible to plan a suitable study to measure the additional "noise turnover". Unfortunately, most of the studies that have been carried out have been concerned almost exclusively with finding the depreciation in the value of residential property due to noise. Incidental to the main study data have been collected on the frequency of sales of residential property in noise-affected areas compared with the "control areas". It would be conven- ient to assume that the samples of house sales used in these studies (Crowley and McClure) are properly representative of the numbers of movements that take place in the two kinds of areas. But we must note first that such data include sales only and not movements of people who rent, secondly some sales data are excluded, such as family sales, on the grounds that they are substantially gifts (these may or may not involve move- ments), and thirdly the authors of such studies do not reveal the size of the population from which they have sampled so it is impossible to get an accurate measure of the percentage move- ment. With all these reservations, therefore, we now review the available evidence.

Crowley's data are summarized in table 6.8. These data comprise the *number* of sales in each year, over the period 1955–69. (Note that unlike McClure's data the observations were not restricted to multiple sales of the same property during the period.) The period has been divided into the pre-jet age up to 1960 and the post-jet period 1961–9.[42] If the number of sales in Area I continued at the same rate as in Area IV, there would have been about 50 sales on average in area I

---

[42] It might be argued that the best dividing line would be 1959–60 since most people would have had their initial experience with jets sometime during this period. Such a division, however, would make little difference to the results.

TABLE 6.8

Average Number of Sales in areas in Toronto

	Airport-affected area (I)	Areas not affected by airport noise (IV)
1955–60	34	94
1961–9	64	139

Source: Crowley (1972), p. 17, Table 3.

during the 1961–9 period. Thus we can adduce that there were 14 excess movements—some 28 per cent above normal. One cannot be sure that all these movements were noise-induced. But there is considerable evidence in the time series of sales in the Crowley data that relatively large numbers of sales were associated with "periods of shock" such as when turbo-jet aircraft were first used. Thus one may take it that aircraft noise was responsible for movements being some 25 per cent above normal.

McClure's data were for houses in the Los Angeles area that had been sold *at least twice* during the period of study 1955–67. They constitute therefore not a sample of sales but rather a sample of *twice-sold* houses. In the four areas analysed by McClure "there were approximately the same number of parcels [of land] in each test area". Thus it is possible to regard the number of two-sales observations as a good indicator of the relative rates of two-sale houses transfers in each area. If, furthermore, it can be assumed that the ratio of multiple sales to movements as a whole is the same in all areas, then we may accept the McClure data as good proxies for movement rates in the areas (however, as we shall see, I do not think this assumption can be sustained). In discussing the noise depreciation data it was argued that the three areas I, II, and III should be classified as noisy. Using this criterion we compare the average

TABLE 6.9

Numbers of Two-or-more Sales, Los Angeles 1955–67

I Very noisy	II Noisy	III Some noise	IV No noise
45	63	36	31

Source: McClure (1969), pp. 9–12.

of the three areas (I, II, and III) with some noise (46) against
the number of observations in the no-noise area (IV). This
suggests therefore that noisy areas have on the average 50
per cent more movers than the quiet area. However, this is an
overestimate because of the fact that with a higher movement
rate in the noisy areas, the incidence of multiple movements
increases even more rapidly.[43] Making a rough allowance for
this sort of bias, the suggestion from McClure's data is that the
true movement rate is between 25 per cent and 30 per cent.[44]
For what it is worth this evidence is consistent with the
figures of Crowley.[45]

We now examine the data available for the London area.
Table 6.10 shows the 'turnover rates' for two areas near
Heathrow—Harlington which is very noisy and Cranford
which is away from the flight path. The turnover rate is the
percentage of houses 'put on sale for a definite period of time'.
Although the sample is very small it was selected from areas
where the aircraft noise was well known and accurately measured. The tentative conclusion is that turnover rates in the noisy
area were between 40 per cent and 50 per cent above those
in the quiet area. Although these are rather higher figures than
the Crowley (Canada) and McClure (USA) data suggest, they
lie well within the sample error from such a small sample
size.[46]

[43] This can be demonstrated by supposing that movements are distributed in
a Poisson form. For the period let us suppose that the mean number of sales
in the noisy areas was 1½ and the mean number in the quiet areas 1. Then the
number of multiple movements will be substantially over 50 per cent more in
the noisy area.

[44] Using the Poisson means of 1·0 and 1·3 for the quiet and noisy areas one
finds that the number of multiple movers in the noisy areas is about 50 per cent
more than those in the quiet areas. But these should be taken as orders of
magnitude only in view of the doubt about the interpretation of the basic
data; in particular we do not know how McClure dealt with triple sales, etc.

[45] It is also important to note that McClure thought that the number of
observations in his sample could be adduced as evidence that "property in the
quiet areas changed hands about 62 per cent as fast in the noisy areas".
Because of the biases discussed above we should reject such an interpretation;
even using his 62 per cent which he obtained by treating area III as quiet,
we should find that the true mean rates are such that the percentage should
be 30–35.

[46] Possible substantive explanations are (1) the greater natural mobility in
the American scene so that movements because of noise bulk less large in the
total, and (2) the larger fraction of (non-controlled) rental properties in
America. These explanations need to be pursued further.

TABLE 6.10

Time period	Harlington (1,052 houses)		Cranford (1,062 houses)	
	Sales	Turnover rate	Sales	Turnover rate
January 68–January 69	31	3·0	21	2·0
January 68–April 69	37	3·6	27	2·5

Source: Cranford–Harlington sales sample collected by the Inland Revenue for the Roskill Commission (1970b).

More extensive information in movement rates—including those in rented property—can be obtained from the 1961 and 1966 population censuses. Donnison (1962) studied the movement of households in 1958 and concluded that 8 per cent of households in England changed houses during a year. From Census data we observe an annual rate of 10·4 per cent between 1961 and 1966 at Hayes (one of the noisy local authority areas near Heathrow). This suggests a noise induced movement rate of some 20 to 30 per cent above the ordinary movement rate.[47]

In *McKennel's study* of noise the respondents were asked questions to elicit whether they 'feel like moving because of aircraft noise'—the results of which are reported, together with the NNI category (Table 6.11). These data are very

TABLE 6.11

NNI	Percentage of people who 'feel like moving because of the noise'
35–45	3·1
45–55	8·0
55 and over	11·0

Source: Wilson Committee (1963), Fig. 16, Appendix.

[47] Some of the moves took place within the local authority area and may have been from very noisy to less noisy houses; we do not know much about such internal migration patterns. We also note that the West London area may have higher rates of natural movement than England and Wales as a whole.

difficult to interpret. If we could trust that the 'feeling' was indeed an intention, then we could interpret the rates as long-term movement rates induced by noise. To check their consistency with the actual data on movements we need to convert the 'feelings' into implied annual movements. Donnison (1962) showed that in England about 25 per cent of people willing to move had in fact moved out in the space of one year. This would give annual movement rates due to noise of 0·8, 2·0, and 2·7 for the three NNI categories during the first year, 0·6, 1·5, and 2·0 for the second year, and so on. These noise movers' rates are somewhat lower than the actual observed rates, but the McKennel study was done early in the jet-age and one must allow for 'mistakes' and the lack of information. The only safe conclusion to draw is that McKennel's data are not dramatically inconsistent with the other observed evidence.

Finally one might at least check to see whether the McKennel data are consistent with the predictions of the noise model. By direct calculations from the Roskill model Gautrin (1973, p. 192) found that, with no differential time-trend in the valuation of noise, the model predicted that the following percentages (Table 6.12) would move because of noise. The

TABLE 6.12

NNI	Percentage moving because of noise—as predicted by model	Percentage who "feel like moving" (McKennel)
35–40	4·0 ⎫	3·1
40–45	5·4 ⎭	
45–50	7·8 ⎫	8·0
50–55	8·5 ⎭	
55+	—	11·0

Note: These are the movements for all price of property.

overall percentages predicted by the model are not dissimilar from those adduced by McKennel in his survey. The most noticeable difference is that the movement rates in McKennel's data increase more sharply with the increase in NNI. Gautrin's predicted movements from the noise model, however, do not take into account the fact that the valuation of a quiet life is expected to rise over time. Were this assumption to be incorporated in the model somewhat higher movement rates would be predicted. Whether the answers to McKennel's questionnaire reflect the expectation of a rising valuation of quiet is not clear. However, it does not seem worth-while to pursue further refinements with such crude data.

It is reasonable to suggest tentatively that the McKennel data and the various other pieces of information on movement rates are not dramatically inconsistent with the predictions of the noise model. I am surprised by the close correspondence between the two sets of figures. But one must add that the model has not really been put through its paces by such empirical evidence; more stringent and critical tests are required.

SOME CONCLUSIONS ON MOVEMENTS DUE TO NOISE

Evidence on the turnover rates of property and in particular residential property is peculiarly scarce, largely because interest has been concentrated on other phenomena. Data have never been collected specifically to analyse the change in turnover rates when a noise nuisance is imposed on an area hitherto quiet. Such data as are available are the by-products of other studies.

When properly interpreted, however, the orders of magnitude of the movements that are attributable to noise are approximately the same in both studies—say between 20 per cent and 30 per cent more movers than there would be under normal non-noisy conditions. There is no evidence of dramatic sustained increases in movement rates—although during certain "shock" years the movements rates may be as much as 50 per cent above normal.

Clearly the data suggest that further analysis of movements rates is well worth pursuing. The aim would be to define more precisely the area and time of impact of the noise nuisance and the dynamics of adjustment of the housing market thereto. Such an inquiry may enable the noise model to be calibrated with respect to observed movement rates.

FURTHER RESEARCH ON NOISE

Perhaps the main impression one derives from the discussion of empirical studies is how little we know of the effects of noise. Much research has been pursued into the physical characteristics, the psychological effects, and physiological consequences of noise; but little has been done to show the consequences on people's decisions about where to live and how much they do in fact pay for a quiet life. I believe that in part this neglect is due to a general distaste for attempts to measure environmental factors in terms of mere money; a distaste sedulously propagated by 'environmentalists' who are anxious to avoid the discovery of the nakedness of their emperor.[48] But I believe that the neglect is largely due to the difficulty of getting data and the complications in analysing the figures. It is possible to solve the problem of the provision of data on the selling prices of houses. In the United Kingdom detailed data on such transactions are maintained by the Inland Revenue. However, the authorities have decided that the information cannot be released under present legislation since publication would compromise the promise of confidentiality. Nevertheless, it seems that after a lapse of some ten years or so the data should be released, perhaps still with detailed addresses and names eliminated, for research on the important problems of amenity valuation etc. Such historical information is unlikely to be used for anyone's commercial gain or loss. And the data would provide reliable benchmarks for many important decisions on public policy.

The other main avenue for research is the actual operation of the property market in a dynamic context. The formal representation of the market where one can buy as much housing as one likes, at the going price, with no transactions costs and with perfect knowledge, is merely a caricature. The elaboration of the adjustment and transactions costs which were incorporated into the noise model constituted some improvement on the simple frictionless model, but it is still a very crude approximation to the actual process. For example, we still cannot explain

---

[48] The arguments run along familiar lines—for example the allegation that since the rich man will pay more for quiet than the poor man, the economist is led to conclude that it is best to provide quiet for the rich rather than the poor; such a conclusion is alleged to be morally offensive, and so to discredit the approach!

the widely observed 'shock' effect when it is alleged to be 'impossible to sell a house' because of the impending airport.[49] Nor have we incorporated the value of knowledge, the learning experience, and the cost of acquiring knowledge into the adjustment process. All these shortcomings emphasize how little we know about the micro-economics of the housing market as it moves from one long-run equilibrium to another.

The simple attractions of the long-run equilibrium results may lead one over-zealously to interpret empirical data too readily as manifestations of the long run. The only inoculation against such a fever of facile interpretation is more evidence on the movement of prices and people over the adjustment period; this is what is signally lacking.

[49] One may interpret this as a voluntary increase in transactions cost—an investment in searching for a buyer—in the expectation that the market will rise.

CHAPTER 7

Policy

THE 'PRICE' APPROACH AND THE 'AUTHORITIES' APPROACH

THE first main purpose of this study is to see whether the economic effects of noise can be analysed with the formal framework of economic theory. But economic theory as such is only a set of 'empty boxes' or a filing system. Our pursuit of empirical evidence in chapter 6 was intended to give content to that filing system, to fill the empty boxes, and to see whether the predictions of theory were consistent with the empirical evidence. While I believe that the observed evidence does conform to the theoretical predictions and that the figures for different surveys are remarkably consistent, whether or not such accumulated evidence should be used for prescriptions of policy is still a matter for judgement. But if the evidence reviewed in chapter 6 is rejected then logically one must accept some alternative analysis and evidence as superior for formulating policy prescriptions. One well-developed alternative basis for decision-making is that of "political attraction"—in its ideal form it is judgement of what "people" will accept and approve. In practice this appears in the form of planning standards and decisions. Even so it is useful to base planning "standards" on the objective evidence of what people are willing to tolerate for certain rewards.

The real question for this chapter is by what *means* these noise assessments should be reflected in policy. Broadly two approaches are possible which we may call the 'price approach' and the 'authorities approach'. (It might be more consistent with current usage to call the 'authorities approach' the 'planning approach'. But the authorities may not be professional planners so it is perhaps better to use the less specific nomenclature.) In the 'price approach' the purpose is to ensure that the quality of residential quiet (a quiet environment) is accorded many of the elements of a property right.

In principle one should try to arrange matters so that those who fly pay for the privilege of taking away the quiet environment of those who live in the noise shadow. Then people would fly only if they were willing to pay for the additional noise nuisance they cause. Airlines would be induced to invest in quiet engines if the pay-off in terms of reduced compensation for noisiness was at least as large as the servicing costs of the investment. If the price of being noisy is right then the amount of air travel and the number of air transport movements and their distribution over the season and time of day will be in the best interests of the community as a whole. Furthermore those who are concerned with the location of airports, whether private or public bodies, will have the appropriate incentive to avoid noise nuisance. In principle the price approach should arrange matters so that the amount paid by air travellers for making noise is received by the residents who suffer. There should be some sort of compensation arrangements for those who, unexpectedly, are deprived of their residential quiet.

The characteristic feature of the price approach is that individuals and airlines are left free to make such contracts and arrangements as they wish provided only that they pay the bill. Unfortunately such an ideal of free contract cannot be extended to the individuals who suffer the noise. While it is true that people can freely choose whether or not to live in the noise shadow, if one does continue to live in the 50–55 NNI zone one cannot *separately* buy peace. The issue is a collective one affecting the whole community.

Such collective or social aspects of decisions about noise have substantially led to the adoption of the 'authorities approach'. This takes the form of specifying standards, embodied either in law or administrative regulation, which prescribe what degree of noise aircraft may make, where and when they may make it, etc.

On noise emission sources these comprise controls on the noisiness of aircraft through certification, specific flight paths, in pilots being required to fly according to noise avoidance procedures, in restricted operations at night, and so on. Probably the main area of control is in airport location—keeping jet aircraft away from centres of population.

9

On noise receivers such regulations take the most common form of land-use zoning to ensure only 'compatible' land uses in the noisy areas. Public purchase of affected property at the 'before-the-noise' market price has also been rather sparingly employed.

The great attraction of the 'price' compared with the 'authorities' approach is that it leaves airlines, airport owners, and the travelling public free to make their own choices. And the noise sufferers and in particular those who are relatively imperturbable have a greater variety of alternatives under the price approach than with the planners' restrictions. The first step in tackling the policy issues on aircraft noise, we suggest, is to arrange the prices so that they reflect the costs imposed on the community. If the landing fees reflected the money value of the disbenefit imposed on the people under the flight paths, then after a suitably long period of adjustment we would be producing the correct mixture of quiet and other goods. Privately owned property would reflect the noise differential in the price, and sites would be adapted to their best use. Noise makers—both proximate and ultimate—would be encouraged to use quiet machines to reduce the landing fee if the saving exceeded the additional costs of being quiet. Similarly the airport authorities would be able to calculate the effects of siting an airport in a populous city and so charging high landing fees and discouraging traffic and revenue compared with siting it in a green field. To get the prices right seems the most significant policy measure that can be undertaken; it is also a highly practical one.[1] True there are additional problems of the distributional effects—to ensure that those whose right to (or at least reasonable expectation of) residential quiet has been expropriated or dashed by airport development are the ones who are compensated. These difficulties of compensation are, however, much easier to solve if the price is right.

Yet the likelihood of airports making the appropriate charges for noise and the even more remote possibility of the airlines

---

[1] Arguments put against using the pricing system to reflect the costs of airports range from the allegation that the authority is bound by some legal red-tape to avoid making large profits to the mutually inconsistent arguments that (1) charging a high landing fee will have no effect on airport usage, and (2) that a high fee will divert planes to other airports. See Walters (1973).

and Civil Aeronautics Board (U.S.A.) or Civil Aviation Authority (U.K.) or Airport Authority adjusting fares in an appropriate way are small. Airports are either entirely governmental
agencies or public or semi-public corporations and they are
very unlikely to exhibit any considerable economic rationality
in their pricing policy.[2] Much of the congestion at existing
airports is due to the combination of a silly policy with respect
to landing fees combined with a reluctance on the part of
government to incur the political cost of visiting a noise and
pollution disbenefit on part of the electorate, and particularly
on marginal constituencies.

It seems regrettable but prudent to assume that one cannot
rely solely on the price approach to provide the appropriate
indicators for both the efficient use of existing airports and
investment decisions in new airports. The "authorities" approach will need to be employed. The authorities may use
regulations and controls which are 'in the public interest'. The
calculations of the economic costs of noise must be made as
part of the cost–benefit study of both the use of the present
airports and the location of new ones. They enable us to judge
how far to go with such regulations and whether they involve
costs which exceed or fall short of the benefits so created.
Unfortunately the use of maximum noise levels as the method of
regulation encourages the design of engines so that they fall
just below the certificated maximum noise emission. It may be
possible to reduce noise considerably below these levels at
small cost; but designers have no incentive to introduce such
quieter engines since they involve albeit small costs but no
corresponding gains.

To summarize, then, the main issues of policy which we
shall examine are: (1) How should one operate existing airports,
taking into account the deleterious effects of noise—in particular how should the landing fees be adjusted to take noise

[2] In the case of the New York Airport system the charges are (1) much too
low, (2) differentiate between airports so that the most congested airports
charge the lowest fees, (3) a consequence of some formulas which were of some
validity years ago before the jet age when there was little congestion, but are
quite wrong now. It may be argued that it would be best to denationalize
airports and allow the private sector to compete with privately developed and
financed airport capacity with freedom to compete for traffic.

into account, and how should quiet planes be allocated between airports? (2) How far should the government go in requiring new aircraft to be 'quiet' and in requiring existing jets to be treated to make them quieter? (3) How can one evaluate in money terms the differential costs of noise of options for the location of a new airport, and, finally, should any existing airport be required to close down because the noise costs exceed the benefit that the airport generates?

AIRPORT CHARGES

Characteristically airport landing charges do increase according to the gross weight of the aircraft—and it is clear that, *ceteris paribus*, the landing fees will at least vary in the same direction as the noise. However, it is very rare to find charges varying according to the noisiness of the aircraft *engines*. Superficially at least such variations seem to be more justifiable than varying the fee according to the weight—at least as far as noise is concerned. Unfortunately there is no simple linear relationship between noisiness of an aircraft on the one hand and the NNI and the relative depreciation of dwellings in noisy areas of the other. This largely arises because, if there are 10 quiet aircraft and 90 noisy ones, one more quiet and one less noisy aircraft will make little difference. But if there are say 95 quiet aircraft and 5 noisy ones, then eliminating the noisy ones and substituting quiet ones will make a lot of difference to the mean PndB. This suggests that the landing fee for noisy aircraft to use an airport which is primarily used by quiet aircraft should be very large indeed. This may be taken as a useful guide for any future restructuring of airport charges.

The present structure of airport charges is most deficient in the fact that charges at different airports for the same aircraft do not reflect the noise costs imposed on the population. In particular, airports near to the urban centres usually have a noise shadow that falls over a very large number of households, whereas competing 'rural' airports affect rather few people. One striking example is the contrast between Washington (D.C.) Dulles and National—the former affects virtually no urban area whereas the latter has flight paths over a substantial fraction of the Metropolitan area. There is therefore a powerful

case for increasing the landing fees at National—and incidentally such a raise would be desirable in any case because of the
relative congestion at National compared with Dulles.

The time is ripe for a review of the whole structure of landing
fees and the financing of airports. In general the landing fees
are determined by the need to cover the costs of the airport
(taking into account such subsidies as are provided by the
Authorities)—to service the debt and to pay for current costs.
Such fees do not adequately reflect the conditions of demand and
do not differentiate between peak periods and off-peak, nor do
they reflect any of the social costs imposed on the community
except in so far as the airport authority formally accepts
responsibility therefore.[3]

Furthermore, the urban airports tend to be the earliest ones
to be developed and so have lower historic costs and, since
they are so convenient, high utilization; all these factors tend
to give low unit accounting costs.[4] But such airports tend to
have very high social costs due to noise. The rural airports,
however, are usually recently built at high accounting cost and,
in spite of their relatively low social cost of noise, their remoteness keeps utilization low. So the landing fees must be high in
order to 'recover' the investment costs. Such a pricing procedure
is precisely the opposite of the best policy! This interesting
problem of landing fees is a very broad one and has many
facets which cannot be further pursued here.

COMPENSATION

The argument that in some way those who suffer from noise
should be compensated for the effects of aircraft flying over
their property has been a bone of legal contention for many
years. Resort to the courts for redress, however, has shown that
under the existing law in the United States and even more so in

[3] Again one must now exclude London from this blanket statement. Some
differential pricing has been introduced and for many years the Authority
has subsidized sound-proofing. See also Walters (1973).

[4] One other possibility which we do not pursue here is that the landing fee
could be varied according to the runway which is used—the noisy highly-
populated approach and take-off paths would cost more than the approach
over water etc. There are obvious difficulties in such a policy measure.

the United Kingdom the proof of damage or nuisance is not easy.[5]

It is tempting to suggest that a law should be promulgated which invests the right of quiet in the property owner. Any abrogation of that right should then be offset by a compensation. The sum of money might be one which is mutually agreeable to the parties. To buy someone's quiet may then be considered a normal market transaction. However, since the incidence of much aircraft noise is largely a consequence of decisions of government agencies, the problem has usually been considered as one of compensation set by law or regulation for injurious affection. The free market approach has not been pursued.

One basic and fundamental difficulty with state compensation would be the need for some sort of grandfather clause. Existing property-owners in noisy houses may have bought their houses at a depreciated price that fully reflects the effects of noise. It would be unjust to compensate such newcomers. Those owners who were caught initially by a 'bolt-from-the-blue' announcement that the airport was going to be established and that the flight paths would go overhead are the obvious losers: only they should be compensated. Anyone who bought his property after the 'bolt-from-the-blue' would purchase at a price which, the market judged, fairly reflected the noise nuisance to come: clearly he should not be compensated. But this line of argument hinges on the unrealistic assumption that the announcement is a bolt-from-the-blue and completely unanticipated. Consider alternatively the realistic assumption where the original owners are to be compensated for the noise but where the information of the airport location (or runway alignment, etc.) leaks out gradually over time. Let us also assume that it leaks out equally to *everyone*: no one gets an inside tip. Finally let us suppose that the compensation is *perfect*—neither undercompensating nor overcompensating the original owners. It follows then that provided the right to compensation is sold as part and parcel of the house there is no reason why the price of the house should change. Perfect

---

[5] For a survey of the legal position in the United States see Lillian R. Altree *et al.* (1968). This study also contains a good economic analysis of noise and the compensation and other problems. For the current position see chapter 6 above.

compensation has retained the old values. But of course we know that *compensation can by its nature never be perfect*, and there is little point in pursuing policies founded on such a false premise. Even if the Authorities in charge of the compensation arrangement accurately judge market price and movement costs, this would overcompensate a few (those who were just about to move anyway) and undercompensate many who would not consider moving even if they were offered market price plus movement cost. There is no administratively feasible system of compensation that can avoid either overcompensation or undercompensation or both.

Knowledge of the Authorities' plans to locate an airport in the chosen spot will be valuable. In the event that, as we assumed above, everyone gets the same amount of knowledge (i.e. there are no insiders) of his loss or gain at the same time, no one can steal an advantage. In the real-world case where knowledge leaks gradually and selectively, speculators with inside knowledge will be able to buy and sell options on appropriate properties. The insiders will gain at the expense of the ordinary citizen who has no such knowledge. Indeed those inside speculators with sufficiently large holdings will often find it profitable to bring political pressure to bear in order to get the best location for their interests.[6] In other words, with any administratively feasible (i.e. non-perfect) system of compensation the distribution of knowledge to insiders will ensure that some of the compensation intended for the ordinary families will be syphoned off.

Such a "leaking" process generates considerable uncertainty about the appropriate 'market price plus moving costs' criterion for compensation. Even with the universal dissemination of knowledge the market price of property affected by the noise shadow is likely to fall relative to property not so affected. And if one attempts to use as a standard the price *before* there was any rumour of an airport at all, one would normally have to go back a very long way. With the complication of insiders first getting information the task of finding a standard would be quite impossible.

Notwithstanding the difficulties of developing proper rules of

---

[6] The deployment of the pro-Foulness lobby during the long saga of locating London's third airport is one example of this process. There are many others.

compensation and in spite of the great transitional problems of adjustment, there does seem to be a case for developing a law to compensate for *new* sources of noise annoyance. The form of compensation should be as simple as possible and preferably based on a rule such as the NDSI and the valuation of the property for purposes of taxation.[7] The NDSI could be fixed by the law for all airports. It would be difficult to vary the NDSI for different levels of house price, so it seems best to have only one standard NDSI. In practice with one NDSI for all houses, whether of the rich or poor, one would find that one was normally overcompensating the lower-income groups and undercompensating the higher-income groups.[8] (This redistributive effect would be consistent with the ostensible views of political parties.) The NNI or CNR contours should be drawn up by an agent independent of the airport authority and monitored on the ground. The airport authority should have the compensation debited to it and should recover such costs by charging aircraft according to the noise nuisance they cause.

One alternative compensation arrangement is to pay the money not to the individual owners but to the local authority that suffers the noise. If the local authority reduced the tax assessments of property owners who were affected by noise in an appropriate way these arrangements would give somewhat similar results to those of direct compensation. But there is no guarantee that the local authority would behave in such an enlightened way, and it seems best to avoid the local authority and deal directly with the individuals affected.

It is worth-while giving some idea of the order of magnitude of the compensation which one might contemplate for a *new* airport. Suppose that the population affected were 20,000 households with an average increase of NNI of 15 (CNR 10)—say an average NNI increase from 30 to 45. If the average price of house were $20,000 (£8,000) the total value of the affected property would be $400 (£160) million. Using an NDSI of 1·0, one would find that the total compensation amounts to $60 (£24) million, and with NDSI = 0·7 the total is $41 (£16)

[7] The owner has an incentive to reduce his tax assessment but to increase his noise compensation. Such a valuation procedure would avoid lengthy assessment cases purely for noise-compensation purposes.

[8] This would not be the case if poor houses were owned by rich landlords. There may then be a case for community compensation—see below.

million. One could make various other assumptions and calculate the associated compensation but we leave that for the
interested reader.[9]

There remains the problem of compensating for movement
costs. If only those who actually move are compensated the
system is more complicated both analytically and administratively. The administration of the scheme requires a time limit
to be specified and a definition of what is a move and sale.
Furthermore, such subsidies to those who move would create
too much mobility since, to the individual owner, moving
becomes costless though it obviously involves real resource
costs. Many additional difficulties would occur with rented
property where the movement costs are largely borne by the
tenant but also partly borne by the owner. Analytically to get
an estimate of the movement costs one must predict the
number of movers. This is a much more difficult task and
subject to much uncertainty.

If on the other hand the authorities compensate people for
movement costs whether they move or not, there will be obvious
elements of inequity. Those who suffer an increase of 25 or 30
in the NNI will be much more likely to move than those who
have suffered only an increase of 10. It seems that the least
inequitable feasible plan is to pay a fixed percentage (about
20 per cent) above the figure given by the NDSI calculation.
Thus in the above case we would add to the $50 (£24) million
another $12 (£5) million disturbance allowance. Such an
arrangement would overcompensate those who are imperturbable and would undercompensate many of those who move
because of the noise; but such inequities are impossible to
avoid.

But it seems to me that it is possible to avoid much of the
political opposition to noise by *deliberately overcompensating*.
For example consider the 20,000 households affected by noise
in London's third airport and imagine a simple rule for compensation as follows: Compensation per head = £20 (NNI-30)

[9] The assumptions we have chosen correspond broadly with the population
affected by the two most desirable inland sites in the London Area. The value
of house, however, corresponds to the scene in the United States. With the
London value of house the compensation would be about halved (i.e. about
£12 million for an NDSI = 1·0). These prices were those of 1967; to get 1973
prices one must multiply by 3 or 4.

for NNI of 35 or over in 5-unit intervals. The family of four in the 45 NNI would get £1,200 and if they were in the 55 NNI the sum would be £2,000. The total cost would be of the order of £25 million, roughly twice the ultimate depreciation of houses. I conjecture, however, that except among the high-income groups who would be undercompensated, such benefi-cence would convert airport opposition into enthusiastic support.

The objection to such open-handed compensation would come from the Treasury which would fear the setting of precedents for such profligacy. Yet, I suspect, it is a mistaken myopic parsimony. The political pressure that accumulates at present often results in not merely costly planning procedures but also in the implementation of very much more costly alternatives. Consider again the case of the Third London Airport, it is conceivable that compensation of the order of £25 million would have reduced the Cublington opposition to impotence if not enthusiastic support—and we should have avoided the many hundreds of millions planned to be spent in the Maplin (Foulness) project. The price system though apparently more expensive is in reality much cheaper than the political system.

Again we have concluded that a simple compensation rule is probably the best that we can achieve. It may be far from the idealists' dream but I believe it is a great improvement on existing arrangements.

We also have the problem of compensation for non-residen-tial property, such as factories, hospitals, schools and various other institutions. The obvious basis for such compensation is insulation costs, where the school etc. would stay in operation. Where it would be necessary or desirable to move reprovision costs are the appropriate figure. Such costs vary enormously and no general rule or figures can be adduced from the evi-dence.[10]

BUYING NOISY HOUSES

Policy prescriptions which try to avoid compensation may try to 'internalise' the otherwise "external" disbenefits of noise. If for example an airport authority actually owned all the property on which noise was inflicted, the noise costs would be debited in the accounts of the authority. It would be

[10] See Roskill Commission (1970a), chapter 21.

hurting itself. Therefore the authority would adequately take
noise costs into account in planning and operating its facility.
The 'expanded firm', as *Albee et al.* (1968) call it, would internalize the noise. The extent of such a foray into real estate by
the airport authority requires careful consideration. In most
cases which have been suggested as practical proposals and at
least partly implemented, the acquisitions have been restricted
to a buffer zone of two miles from the runway threshold.[11]
This deals with only the very few who suffer a lot, it does not
help the many who suffer moderately or a little—more than a
million people or a quarter of a million households in the case of
Heathrow. Clearly to be effective the 'expanded' firm must
incorporate many properties and much land.

If the 'expanded firm' concept were applied to existing airports where the noise nuisance is most pressing, it would
involve setting up airport real estate authorities of truly
mammoth dimensions. If for example one applied the concept
to Heathrow *and* if one limited the properties acquired to the
45 NNI and over, one would still have 80,000 households falling
into the zone of the 'expanded firm'. The capital value of the
residential property alone would be of the order of $1,200
million (£480 million). (To include the 35–45 NNI would add
another $8 (£3·2) billion.[12] And the costs of free acquisition of
such property would be larger than this by some 25–50 per cent.)

The costs involved in such a change of ownership would
almost certainly outweigh the long-term net benefits (if any)
over any other alternative scheme. But even if that were not so,
the creation of new large corporations would inevitably involve
serious risks of inefficiency. Public corporations and government departments have a poor record of property development
and management.[13] For example, attempts by road authorities
to internalize the appreciated site values of road construction

---

[11] See *Roskill Report*, p. 146. The experience of Los Angeles International is
also of interest here.

[12] There are 700,000 households or 2,800,000 people affected by noise of 35
NNI or higher. See *Roskill Report*, p. 60.

[13] British Rail, the various Dock Authorities, and other public corporations
do not appear to attract the flair and insights that property developers need.
But it should also be added that such corporations are often constrained either
explicitly by law or some administrative process or implicitly by political
pressures. The waste of publicly owned land is not necessarily the corporation's
or Department's fault.

have normally failed.[14] The crucial argument, however, is that such an enormous corporation would be too great a concentration of economic power and too large an equity to escape over-all government control and regulation and all the inefficiencies of such political oversight. The case of the fossilized railroads should be recalled.

These arguments, however, apply with much less force to new airports. Potential airport sites nowadays are located away from dense populations so that few people in existing houses are affected by the new source of noise. For example with only 5,000 properties to be acquired the cost at $20,000 (£8,000) per house is $100 (£40) million, and if we add on the land value the cost may be thought to be the order of $200 (£80) million. This may be about 20 per cent of the total capital invested in a new airport. The real difficulty, however, with a green-field site is that property values respond sensitively to rumours of airport development. A suitable standard equitable to the expropriated owner is difficult to obtain. The normal method of valuation—market value in its existing use—would be grossly unfair to those owners of the acquired property who would be excluded from sharing in the vast appreciation brought about by the airport rumours. One alternative blanket approach would be for the airport authority to acquire *all* sites within near proximity of the airport so that the monetary advantages of accessibility recently conferred are appropriated by the agency that brings them about—the airport authority. But this takes us back to the mammoth corporation and all the objections thereto. One may conclude therefore that the 'expanded firm' approach is more appropriate for new green-field airport sites than for existing sites. But there are considerable and I believe overriding difficulties of any major acquisition programme.

THE NOISE COST OF AN AIRCRAFT MOVEMENT
AND ECONOMIES OF SCALE

The detailed calculation of the effect of noise on the time series of property values and movements is a long and complicated

---

[14] One well-documented early example of this was the development of Strand and Kingsway in London. See Ralph Turvey (1953/4). Professor Yoram Barzel has pointed out that the real explanation of such failures is the absence of any incentive to maximize profits.

business to which we return later in this chapter. But it is worth-while examining some of the implications of the figures to find the effects of an aircraft movement on the gross depreciation of a typical house and so on the total depreciation generated over the whole noise shadow.

It is naturally tempting to calculate the effects of an aircraft movement on *gross* depreciation of house prices again assuming certain levels of operation and certain numbers and types of households affected. To be specific let us assume: 20,000 households affected—let us suppose over 40 NNI £10,000 or $25,000 is the value of each house; $N = 500$—this corresponds to a very busy airport indeed; NDSI(NNI) = 1·0. Then we can calculate the total gross noise depreciation due to an additional movement: since one additional movement adds 15/500 to NNI, and one NNI reduces by 1·0 per cent the value of the house, to find total gross depreciation we multiply by the number of houses so affected and the value of each house. Thus we find that total additional depreciation (gross) is

$$\frac{15}{500} \times \frac{1 \cdot 0}{100} \times 25{,}000 \times 20{,}000 = \$150{,}000 \quad \text{or} \quad £60{,}000 \ approx.$$

This represents the capitalized present value of an additional aircraft movement every day. For an aircraft movement therefore this gives a capitalized value of about $430 (£172)—which at an interest rate of 10 per cent is equivalent to about $43 (£17) per annum. This figure then represents the aggregate annual *gross* cost in property depreciation per aircraft movement.

One can explore changes in the basic assumptions to find their effects. For example if one had about 80,000 households affected and each of them were priced at about $13,000 (£5,000), then using the income elasticity of 2·0 we would get approximately the same result. It must be noted, however, that 500 aircraft movements is unrealistically large for one runway during the daylight hours of a summer's day, so these figures for marginal depreciation in fact explore only the *lower* limits. Taking a more typical figure for mixed operations (landing and take-off on one runway), a householder may hear of the order of 100 aircraft per busy day. If there were only 100 aircraft per

day then the effect would be to multiply the marginal depreciation by 5, so that the landing and take-off would each cost
$215 (£86).

This example illustrates an important result for policy
purposes: *there are substantial economies of scale in aircraft
noise*. In practical terms this means that the nuisance generated
by one runway handling 400 air movements a day is considerably less than that generated by two runways with 200 movements a day each (if the numbers of people affected are the
same for all runways). Concentration of noise is a "good thing".
This result is adduced from the evidence that a unit of NNI
or CNR is priced at approximately the same value—so that a
unit increase in NNI or CNR is about as "bad" whether one is
due to increased PndB or to numbers of wherever it occurs on
the scale. As the number of aircraft increases, however, the
effect on NNI and CNR becomes less and less, since:

$$d(NNI)/dN = 15/N, \qquad d(CNR)/dN = 10/N.$$

Thus when $N = 50$ an extra aircraft adds 0·3 to NNI and 0·2
to CNR but when $N = 500$ the corresponding additions are
only 0·03 and 0·02. The results can be used in practical cases to
answer the following question: suppose we are faced with the
possibility of transferring one flight from a congested (500)
downtown airport affecting 20,000 households to an uncongested
(100) rural airport affecting only 10,000 households (assumed
equally wealthy). We can easily see that although the number
of households so affected is halved the low number count means
that the noise at the rural airport is 5 times more annoying and
so has a 2½-fold effect on depreciation. This figure should then
be compared with the congestion costs so avoided and any
additional access costs.[15]

It should be stressed that we have measured here only the
gross depreciation due to noise. We should also expect there to

---

[15] This rationalizes a common complaint about economic analysis that it
concentrates on the marginal conditions and ignores the global effects. For
example reducing the number of aircraft by one when there are 500 flying
has very little impact on NNI, but reducing the 500 to zero has much more
than 500 times the impact of one. It is not enough to get the marginal conditions right, we must also ensure that it is worthwhile for all 500 to take to the
air. In other words we must ask the question: Is there a need for a new airport
at all? This is taken up later.

be a gross appreciation of houses which have not suffered any increment in noise, so we have not calculated the *net* effect on all property values (or the net income of landlords as a class) of increasing noise. Neither have we taken into account the effect on property values, whether noisy or not, of additional accessibility associated with the property due to the additional airline service. The *net* effect on property values will take all these other effects into account. The gross depreciation does not. It should also be stressed that the NNI does not take into account variations in the fraction of night to day flights—so it is not sensible to use these data to discuss the allocation of flights between day and night. More sophisticated measures such as the NEF could be developed to take this factor into account.

HEAVIER AIRCRAFT AND NEW ENGINES

One of the main efforts of the authorities approach has been to certify engines in terms of their noise performance in relation to weight. So far we have discussed the effects of a 'standard' aircraft—the addition of which does not affect the $\overline{\text{PndB}}$, so that all we needed to take into account was the addition to the number. But it is known that heavier aircraft using the same technology have a higher PndB than lighter jets; in fact a doubling of the weight of an aircraft will add 3 PndB to its noise propogation. Similarly the effects of the new engines with the high bypass ratio is to reduce the PndB for the same weight by 10 units. The effect on mean PndB can be calculated from the formula:

Reduction in $\overline{\text{PndB}}$ if the fraction of quite planes is $p =$

$$= 10\log\left(\frac{1}{1-0\cdot9p}\cdot\text{PndB}\right).$$

(See Roskill Commission (1970a), §§ 18–25.)

To divert from the main discussion, it is worth noting in this connection that the forecasts of future noise take into account both the increase due to the employment of heavier aircraft and the decrease due to the increasing use of the quieter engines

with the high bypass ratio.[16] The precise mix of heavier aircraft
and quiet engines will determine the net effect. The consequences
for Heathrow have been calculated with some precision and
are shown in Figure 7.1. It will be observed that from the
1975 to 1981 the PndB will be very high. Then there will be a
dramatic decline over the next decade or so.

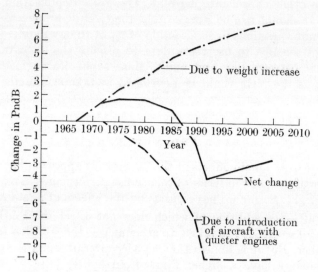

FIG. 7.1. Roskill forecast of noise at Heathrow.

To return to the specific weight/engine effect, from the above
formulas we can calculate the effects of increasing the number
of quiet aircraft from zero per cent to 15 per cent—this reduces
the mean PndB by 0·6, and so we can trace the effects of NNI,
and then, through the NDSI (NNI), on property values.

These results again emphasize an important point for policy.
It is best to concentrate quiet aircraft on one airport (runway),
and especially where the number of households affected is very

[16] Since these calculations were carried out, there has been an accumulation
of additional evidence which suggests that (a) the larger and quieter aircraft
are being introduced rather more rapidly than was assumed by the Roskill
Commission, and (b) engines are likely to be more quiet than was assumed by
the Commission. Both of these amendments affect the noise predictions for
the 1980s, and (increasingly) the 1990s.

large. Spreading them around and mixing them with pre-
dominantly noisier aircraft will be less efficacious.

RETROFIT AND QUIET AIRCRAFT

Retrofit is a method of making noisy jets rather more quiet.
It is tempting therefore to use the data to evaluate whether
the owners of noisy property could conceivably find it worth
their while to finance the costs of retrofitting all the existing
aircraft fleet. It has been suggested that in order to retrofit the
existing fleet of the United States airlines an expenditure of
about $2 billion would be required—and perhaps there would
be additional costs of reduced range, greater maintenance, etc.
Let us accept the $2 billion as an appropriate order of magnitude.
It seems that a rather conservative estimate of the number of
people affected by aircraft noise in the United States would be
some 4 million—probably more than one million households.[17]
Taking the average price of house at $20,000 and using an
NDSI of 0·7, we find that house-owners would be willing to
pay up to $1·4 billion. From such a 'back-of-the-envelope'
calculation one would very tentatively conclude that there is
certainly no overwhelming case for retrofitting the whole
United States fleet.[18] Even if one did a more careful study
taking into account the many effects we have ignored, such as
the fact that relieving a household of noise it has suffered for
some time confers less benefit than the costs of imposing noise
upon a household hitherto quiet (see below), it would be doubt-
ful if any overriding case would emerge for retrofitting. But
the question is well worth further investigation.

There is also the closely related problem of the development
of STOL (short take-off and landing) and VTOL (vertical take-
off and landing) aircraft. Such aircraft dramatically reduce the
area affected by noise. But, with present technology, although
they use less runway per air movement, STOL and VTOL use
more airspace per passenger carried than do conventional jets

---

[17] Obtained by assuming that the 20 major airports affect an average of at
least 30,000 families in 40+NNI—and then adducing the remainder for the
other airports.

[18] Note that we are enormously simplifying the problem since it has important international connotations and very wide-ranging effects. Furthermore, as
Professor Yoram Barzel has pointed out, when the absolute numbers are as
large as these, it is very likely that it would be worthwhile to search for
intermediate solutions. The net gains are likely to be large in absolute size.

and the costs of operation seem to be some 30–40 per cent above
those of the competing 'airbus'. There is, however, so much
uncertainty about an intensive STOL or VTOL operation that
the trade-offs between cost increases and noise reduction are
not even remotely discernible. One hopes, however, that the
building blocks we have suggested may be useful in any future
assessment.

DECREASING AND INCREASING NOISE—AN
ASYMMETRY

For the most part the authorities have been concerned only
with increasing noise—for the obvious reasons that over the
past decades this has been the main effect of the rapid growth
of air traffic, and of course people complain about more noise.
One rarely hears about *decreasing* noise. Only occasionally is a
community given a respite—as flight paths are changed or
noise avoidance procedures pursued.

There is a considerable asymmetry in the effects of increasing
and reducing noise. An area that is noisy and has been noisy
for some time will have acquired more than its share of imperturbables, and insulation costs of a once-and-for-all variety will
have already been incurred. If the noise can be reduced by
10 Pndb then there will be some gain. But such a gain will be
considerably less than the loss which would be imposed on a
community suffering an *increase* of 10 PndB in noise. Unfortunately we have little knowledge of a reaction from a
community enjoying a decrease in noise. Most of our knowledge
and virtually all the figures in chapter 6 have been derived from
people who have suffered increases in the amount of noise. But
it is reasonable to use these values in present policy discussions
because for almost a decade the problem will be one of reducing
the rate of increase of noise—not reducing the level.

It will be noticed also that there is not likely to be any
suggestion that those who enjoy a reduction in noise should pay
for the improvement in their environment. Such an appreciation of their property is a windfall gain to the owners. In some
cases, however, it may be represented as the return on an
expensive investment of time and money in political lobbying.
The misdirection of resources both in airport investment and in

political activity is the cost of the politicization of these decisions.

ZONING

The main reaction of authorities to a new noise source is so-called zoning—or perhaps directly controlling development. Typically for the noisiest areas (say over 50 NNI) all residential building is banned, or perhaps only urgent infilling is allowed. Buildings are allowed which are deemed to have compatible uses—such as certain types of industry (drop-forging works)—and zoning restrictions (or development certificates) are allocated accordingly. The most casual view of airports, which the air passenger may see by looking out of the window, suggests that such zoning restrictions are not strikingly success-ful; much new development apparently does take place within the noisy areas. This testifies to the high demand for noisy residential property in the vicinity of airports, as well as to the ingenuity of builders and buyers in avoiding planning re-strictions. People are willing to spend a considerable amount of time and money in bending the zoning restrictions to get a noisy house with nice accessibility. One would therefore imagine that this evidence may be deployed as an argument—and perhaps a powerful argument—against zoning restrictions. Why not permit the imperturbables to build and live in the noisy areas and so capitalize on the advantages of such access-ibility? If we do not allow them to settle there valuable residential sites are being wasted.

The arguments which have been put against this free market solution have usually hinged on the belief that the efficacy of a free market supposes that there is 'perfect information'. Many people, it is said, buy a house in an area not knowing that it is to become noisy; some persons 'do not appreciate' the seriousness of aircraft noise when they buy a house in a noisy area. They must be protected against themselves; and even if it were true that imperturbables could easily stand the noise their children must be protected by the state's prescription.

Such arguments cannot be construed as against the free market solution as such. They merely imply that there should be greater dissemination of information about aircraft noise. The airport authority should be required to post information about expected flight and approach paths and runway use well in advance.[19] Noise measurement techniques are now sufficiently advanced to make such procedures quite practical and even cheap. The airport authorities should be required to stick to their forecast operational pattern and only if there are emergencies or very large technological advantages from switching would this be allowed (perhaps with penalty payment). There are great advantages in being conservative and having very few changes. It may well be possible for the airport authority to be required to give notification of noise contours for periods up to five years hence—and to pay 'penalties' for any deviation between forecast and outcome. But all these arguments for better information do not imply that 'the state must protect them from themselves'. A person may take too rosy a view of the effects of aircraft noise just as he may be unduly optimistic about the house foundations being sound: it is, however, his responsibility by the general principle of *caveat emptor*.[20] The job of the state is to protect the individual from misrepresentation by the airport authority and to ensure a stability in the authorities' behaviour. If an imperturbable wishes to live in the noisy area, well knowing what the consequences are, then there is no reason why the state should prevent him from doing so. By zoning the state throws away valuable resources in the form of highly accessible residential sites.[21] It seems that in the

[19] It will nevertheless be clear that in principle the dissemination of information should normally be performed by the private sector. If such information can be profitably acquired and sold then some private firm will be set up to perform this function. For example estate agents (realtors) who have a good track record in giving advice about future aircraft movements will normally command more business than those who are poor predictors. But it may well be argued that the process of private enterprise in collecting and selling such information will be painfully slow. Public statements by the Authorities will be more efficient.

[20] The argument that the imperturbable's children must be protected by the state against the parent's decisions is not one that should commend itself to the free society.

[21] It is often said that people move into an area well knowing about the noise and then proceed to campaign to get the noise stopped by closing down runways etc. Such people will often claim that they 'never knew it would be like this' and are a familiar bugbear to airport authorities. Such behaviour, however, is perfectly rational, if not entirely unreprehensible, since a closure of the offending runway may well increase the value of their property by thousands of dollars. A little political pressure may be a small price to pay for such a windfall gain.

United States zoning has had only a marginal effect on the
actual outcome.[22] In Britain certainly the effects of planning on
airports such as Heathrow have been small so far. The current
climate of opinion, however, suggests that planning controls
may be much more virorously enforced in future airport
locations. This seems to me to be an unfortunate development.

NEW AIRPORTS—COST/BENEFIT OF NOISE

The use of the value-of-quiet calculations in determining the
location of new airports is both important and complicated.
The costs of new airports consist of various so-called tangible
costs, such as the costs of clearing and levelling the site, con-
structing the runways, etc., and intangible costs, such as noise,
destruction of other amenities (visual intrusion), and so on.[23]
Probably noise is the most important of the intangibles that
enters into the calculation of cost benefit studies of airports.

The problem now is to calculate the amount of money that
would *just* compensate people for the intrusion of noise.[24] A
first approximation is the depreciation in house values. And
this would be a very good approximation if moving costs were
trivial and housing "units" including all associated amenities
were homogeneous entities available at a fixed price on the
market. Such assumptions are, however, manifestly absurd.
In order to measure the costs incurred we must construct a
model that *predicts* the number of movers due to noise and the
number that stay put and suffer the noise—then the costs of
movement can be incorporated in the calculation.

The model, as described in chapter 5 above, is very complex
in its operational form. The essence of the calculations is,

[22] See M. H. Yeates (1965), and John Delaphons (1962), chapter IV.

[23] It is usually represented that the tangible costs are easy to ascertain with
a high degree of certainty, whereas the intangible costs are difficult to measure
with any acceptable degree of confidence. Such a view is mistaken. The
uncertainties associated with tangible costs, such as those of construction,
may be very large indeed and perhaps larger than those associated with noise
costs. Concorde is an interesting example.

[24] The proposition that different people will have different marginal utilities
of income and that therefore, to get a utility measure, one must weight any
money gain or loss with the marginal utility is one that has been much debated
in the literature and in the Roskill Hearings and will not be pursued here.

however, simple, and is explained in the following table:
(See also Roskill Papers and Proceedings Vol. VII p. 376).

Action	Costs
(1) Move because of noise	(a) Differential surplus
	(b) Costs of moving
	(c) Depreciation due to noise
(2) Natural move	Depreciation due to noise
(3) Stay put	Value of noise annoyance
(4) Move *into* noisy area	No disbenefit and any net benefit not counted.

The Roskill Commission made several critical assumptions
about the valuation of noise nuisance by individual households
and the changes in that value over time. The assumption of
dominant effect was that the valuation of noise nuisance would
increase over time at 5 per cent per annum. This value appears
to be consistent with the evidence on income elasticities and the
expected growth of incomes.[25]

Running the complete model for the four sites considered by
the Commission gives results from which the data in table 7.1
have been derived. Column 3 of the table shows the mean value
of NNI which the number of households over 35 NNI were expected to suffer, and column 4 gives the variance. Column 5
shows the *total* NNI units inflicted on the population in the over
35 NNI areas (and is obtained by multiplying the mean NNI by
the number of households); this measures the total noise nuisance in terms of NNI units. Although there is no natural 'zero'
on the NNI scale it is reasonable to assume that at 27 NNI in
country areas with low ambient noise levels no one would be
annoyed by the aircraft. Consequently we have calculated the
total increase in NNI over the base line of 27, and this is shown
in column 6. Column 7 shows the noise cost for each site as
obtained from the detailed noise model. Column 8 shows the
noise cost per unit NNI over 27 (i.e. column 7 divided by
column 6).[26]

[25] In general I believe there was a tendency to overvalue noise in the Roskill
model.

[26] The noise costs have been discounted to 1982 on the argument that this
date lies somewhere near the middle of the time range of disbursements for the
construction of the airport.

TABLE 7.1

Residential noise costs

(1) Site	(2) Number of households of 35 NNI or more (000s)	(3) Mean NNI	(4) Variance of NNI	(5) Total NNI (000s)	(6) Total NNI above 27 (000s)	(7) Noise Cost (1982 present value)	(8) Noise Cost per NNI above 27
Cublington	29·4	42·1	4·29	1,238	444	22·7	51·1
Thurleigh	25·6	42·4	8·05	1,066	394	15·6	39·6
Nuthampstead	94·8	40·2	2·46	3,811	1,251	72·2	57·8
Foulness	20·3	41·8	3·51	849	301	10·2	33·9

Source: Roskill Report and calculations of author.

A SIMPLE RULE

Column 8 shows that there is considerable variation in the cost per unit NNI over 27. Part of this is easily explained by the fact that the sites have different variances of NNI. For example Thurleigh, although it has a lower total NNI count than Cublington (col. 5), has a much higher variance, and this is mainly due to the fact that 1,890 Thurleigh households lie in the 55+NNI whereas only 226 Cublington household are above 55. In these high NNI contours households can be expected more readily to move to avoid the noise and imperturbables will take their place. Thus the high noise costs are reduced by the opportunity for movement out of the area. The variance of the NNI reflects the extent to which one may avoid the noise costs by moving. In fact, as can be seen in diagram where the cost per unit NNI (over 27) and the variance of NNI have been plotted for the three inland sites there is a simple linear relationship between cost per unit NNI and the variance. The rule may be expressed as follows:

> Cost per
> unit NNI = 65·6 − 3·5 (variance NNI) *minus* 27
> in £

Foulness seems to be a marked exception to this rule. But appearances are deceptive, since the traffic build-up at Foulness was assumed to be considerably less rapid than at the three inland sites and consequently the costs are discounted over a longer period. Rough calculations suggest that if an allowance is made for the delayed build-up the Foulness observation would lie near the line.

The simplicity of this formula is one of its greatest assets since one may avoid the costs of running the full model on each occasion an estimate of noise costs is needed. The procedure is:

(1) find the numbers in NNI contours:
(2) calculate total NNI and variance of NNI;
(3) forecast cost per unit NNI from formula;
(4) apply cost per unit to total NNI to find total noise cost.

It must be remembered that this model's numerical results apply to an airport which is announced in 1971 and opens its

first runway in 1982. A shorter lead period would increase costs
somewhat. Similarly it is dated in 1968 pounds and allowance
must be made for inflation.

THE GENERAL APPLICATION OF THE ROSKILL MODEL

The full Roskill noise model has not been applied to airports
in the United States. The question whether it would give very
different results or not can be really resolved only by trying it
out. There are, however, some grounds for supposing that the
answers in terms of cost per unit NNI or CNR may not be very
different from those obtained for the London sites. We know
that the NDSIs are similar from the review of the evidence in
chapter 6. The rate of natural movers in the United States is
rather greater than in England and this would tend to reduce
the noise costs in the United States. However, this would be
offset in some degree by the higher average value of house—
perhaps about 65–70 per cent more in the United States.
I conjecture therefore that the results would be broadly the
same. This suggests, therefore, that my *simple* model may be
used to give a rough approximation to the costs.

We can also check the order of difference between the rough
estimate of house-price depreciation from the NDSI calculations and the model's cost figures. Taking the total number of
NNI units over 27 as 444,000 at Cublington and valuing the
average house at £5,000 using an NDSI of 1·0 we would get a
total house price depreciation of about £22 million. This is,
accidentally, very close to the figure of the noise model. Using
the same data for Thurleigh gives a figure of £19 million which
is more than 20 per cent above the noise cost model figure (for
reasons which we mentioned above). The crude depreciation
figures miss the subtleties of the differences between sites that
are picked out by the noise model, but they are of the right
order of magnitude.

A superficial view of these noise costs may be that they are
"too small" and perhaps only about 10–20 per cent of the
capital cost of the airport. But our intuition is conditioned by
our experience of the existing badly sited airports—such as
National in Washington, J. F. Kennedy in New York, and
Heathrow in London—which affect 10 or even 30 times the

number of people that a green-field site would affect. The difference is indeed an order of magnitude.

The next question is naturally: Can one use the noise cost model for predicting the benefits which would flow from *reducing* noise levels around existing airports—or conceivably from closing airports down completely and eliminating virtually all aircraft noise? It is tempting to suppose that all one has to do is to make the costs into benefits and proceed as before, simply put the model into reverse and run it. However, this is clearly not the case, for the following reasons:

(1) Certain investments will have been incurred (such as soundproofing) which cannot be disinvested or recovered (see above).
(2) While in the case of increasing noise the additional nuisance and moving costs were *both* debited to the noise increase, in the case of a noise *decrease* the noise reduction is credited but the movement costs and surplus loss are still debited—these are the costs of change *per se* whether for better or for worse.

The benefits of closing down an airport—and particularly if it is a large airport and has been established for many years as a jet airport—will be considerably less than the costs of establishing one, reckoned as an average per household affected or as a cost per unit NNI change. This can be observed when we set out the reactions of persons in the noise model to a decrease in noise.

(1) Stay put and enjoy the quiet if the value of the quiet exceeds the appreciation of the house less the surplus and removal costs which would be lost by moving or, in symbols

$$V(\Delta q) > A - R - S$$

(where V is the value of the change in quiet and A is the appreciation in the price of the house).
(2) Move out of newly quiet area to noisy area if

$$V(\Delta q) < A - R - S.$$

(3) Move out of area for reasons other than the new peace
(4) Move *into* newly quiet area.

The net benefits associated with these categories can be set out in the usual way; but we not that R and S appear with a *negative* sign indicating that they are costs which must be offset against the benefits of the new peace.

This model has not been applied to any existing airport closure—partly because questions of closing them down are usually only of academic interest and, notwithstanding the bitter attacks of environmentalists and custodians of the sectional interests of the property-owners, the complete cessation of flights from airports such as Heathrow, J. F. Kennedy, Los Angeles International, etc., is quite impossible. Nevertheless, the taste for evocative, if irrelevant, figures which tell us what would be the benefits from closing down Heathrow, J. F. Kennedy, etc., is so great that some sort of response is needed. Making some rough adjustments, but debiting movement costs etc., and by allowing somewhat lower values for the NDSIs associated with Heathrow, one would obtain a figure in the region of £100 million (at 1982 present value, 1970 prices) if it were announced in 1972 that Heathrow would cease operations with effect from 1982. This figure is very tentative indeed and I would not be surprised if a full-scale study gave results either as low as £50 million or as high as £150 million. It is important, however, to stress that one cannot extrapolate from the new-airport-green-fields-site case. For example, we know that Heathrow affects about nine times as many people as would Nuthampstead, but it would be silly to estimate the benefits of closing Heathrow as nine times the costs of Nuthampstead (i.e a collosal £720 million!). The problem and the answers are quite different.

CONCLUDING COMMENTS

There is no doubt that many people will find the treatment of noise in these chapters objectionable or even offensive. To some the right of residential quiet is a fundamental human right; and each person should get his due share of peace and there should be no thought of trading quiet on the market place. Yet a little reflection will show that, even if it were possible (and it is not!) to prevent such selling of quiet for money, it would be un-desirable. The market expands choice and permits each individual freely to express his preferences. The state should try to encourage the existing market in quiet, not attempt to suppress it.

Of course the analysis of the market for quiet is in its infancy. The numerical results adduced in this study must be treated with a mixture of caution and scepticism. The analytical results may be claimed to be oversimplified and naïve. This study is merely a start. I believe that the general methodology can be applied to other environmental problems such as traffic noise and pollution. These problems can be brought under the searching probe of economic analysis and at least one may hope that less bad policies will be pursued.

BIBLIOGRAPHY

ALTREE, LILLIAN R., *et al.*, 'Legal Aspects of Airport Noise and Sonic Boom', mimeograph (Stanford, 1968); *Journal of Law and Economics* (Chicago), 15 (1972).

BECKER, GARY S., 'Irrational Behaviour and Economic Theory', *Journal of Political Economy*, 70 (Feb. 1962).

COLMAN, ALLAN H., 'Aircraft Noise Effects on Property Values', Environmental Standards Circular, City of Inglewood, California (Feb. 1972).

CROWLEY, R. W., 'The Effects of an Airport on Land Values', Working Paper A.72.4, Minister of State, Urban Affairs, Ottawa (1972).

DELAPHONS, JOHN, *Land Use Controls in the United States* (Cambridge, 1962).

DONNISON, D. 'The Movement of Households in England', *Journal of the Royal Statistical Society*, Series A, 125 (1962).

DYGERT, PAUL K., and DAVID SANDERS, 'On Measuring the Cost of Noise from Subsonic Aircraft', Institute of Transportation and Traffic Engineering, mimeograph (Berkeley, 1972).

EMERSON, FRANK C., 'The Determinants of Residential Value with Special Reference to the Effects of Aircraft Nuisance and other Environmental Features', Ph.D. thesis, University of Minnesota (1969).

GALLOWAY, William J., and DWIGHT E. BISHOP, *Noise Exposure Forecasts: Evolution Evaluation Extensions and Use Interpretations*, Department of Transportation, Federal Aviation Authority Office of Noise Abatement, mimeograph (Aug. 1970).

GAUTRIN, J. F., 'The Economics of Aircraft Noise', Ph.D. thesis, University of London (1973).

HALL, THOMAS H. III, and WILLIAM R. BEATON, 'A Factor Formula for Valuation of Aviation Easements', *Appraisal Journal*, 33.1 (Jan. 1965).

HART, P. E., 'Population Densities and Optimum Flight Paths', *Regional Studies*, 7 (1973).

KRYTER, KARL, *Journal of the Acoustical Society of America*, 31 (1959).

DE LEEUW, FRANK, 'The Demand for Housing: a Review of Cross-section Evidence', *Review of Economics and Statistics*, 53.1 (Feb. 1971).

McCLURE, PAUL T., 'The Effect of Jet Noise on the Value of Real Estate', American Institute of Aeronautical Acoustics Paper (1969).

Noise Advisory Council, *Aircraft Noise: Should the Noise Number Index be Revised* (HMSO, 1972).

PAIK. INJA KIM, 'Impact of Transportation Noise on Urban Residential Property Value with Special Reference to Aircraft Noise', Consortium of Universities, Washington D.C., mimeograph (1970).

PAUL, MARGARET, 'Can Aircraft Noise Nuisance be Measured in Money?', *Oxford Economic Papers*, 23 (Nov. 1971).

Roskill Commission, *Report of the Commission on the Third London Airport (Chairman: The Hon. Mr. Justice Roskill)* (HMSO, 1971). (Cited in text as *Roskill Report*.)

———, *Commission on the Third London Airport, Papers and Proceedings Stage III*, vol. vii, part 2: *Results of Research Team's Assessment* (HMSO, 1970). (Cited in text as Roskill Commission, 1970a.)

———, *Commission on the Third London Airport, Papers and Proceedings*, Stage V, Evidence Days 49–63: Public Hearings, mimeograph. (Cited in text as Roskill Commission, 1970b.)

———, Further Research Team Work Papers, mimeograph (1970). (Cited in text as Roskill Commission, 1970c.)

TURVEY, RALPH, 'Recoupment as an Aid in Financing Nineteenth-Century Street Improvements in London', *Review of Economic Studies*, 21(1), no. 54 (1953/4).

WALTERS, A. A., 'Mrs. Paul on Aircraft Noise—A Correction', *Oxford Economic Papers*, 24 (July 1972).

———, 'Investment in Airports and the Economist's Role', in *Cost Benefit Analysis and Cost Effectiveness*, ed. J. N. Wolfe (London, 1973).

Wilson Committee, *Final Report of the Committee on the Problem of Noise*, Cmnd. 2056 (HMSO, 1963).

YEATES, M. H., 'The Effect of Zoning on Land Values in American Cities; a Case Study', in *Essays on Geography in Honour of Austin Miller*, ed. J. B. Whitton and P. D. Wood (Reading, 1965).